PRACTICE FOR CAMBRIDGE
CAMBRIDGE
FIRST CERTIFICATE in ENGLISH

SET TWO

Margaret Archer   Enid Nolan-Woods

Nelson

Nelson English Language Teaching
100 Avenue Road
London NW3 3HF

An International Thomson Publishing Company

London • Bonn • Boston • Madrid • Melbourne • Mexico City • New York • Paris • Singapore • Tokyo

First published by Nelson ELT, a division of Thomas Nelson and Sons Ltd

ISBN 0-17-555566-4

NPN   19 18 17 16 15 14 13 12

Printed in China

ÀCKNOWLEDGEMENTS
The publishers are grateful to the following for permission to reproduce copyright material. They have tried to contact all copyright holders, but in cases where they may have failed will be pleased to make the necessary arrangements at the first opportunity.

University of Cambridge Local Examinations Syndicate for the specimen answer sheet; Hutchinson Publishing Group Ltd for an extract from *Slow Boats to China* by Gavin Young; Sightline Publications Ltd for an adapted extract from 'Rent a Droid' by John Biggins in *Next* (December 1983) and an extract from 'Frankenstein in LA' by Peter Rondinone in *Omni* (Volume 6, Number 2); Godfrey Davis Europcar Ltd for an extract from their van rental leaflet; International Baccalaureate Office for their information leaflet; Neil Allen and Penguin Books Ltd for an extract from *The Puffin Book of Athletics* (Puffin Books 1980) pp. 42–3, copyright © Neil Allen 1980, reprinted by permission of Penguin Books Ltd; Headway Publications Ltd for 'Arriving at London Heathrow Airport' and an extract from 'About your flight' in *British Airways High Life* (September 1983); Ramblers' Association for an extract from their leaflet 'How Shall I Find the Way?'; Oxford University Press for an extract from *Lark Rise to Candleford* by Flora Thompson (1954); The Polytechnic of Central London Languages Library for an extract from their library leaflet; Dolphin Activities Ltd for an extract from their residential adventure holidays brochure; B.E.D. Exhibitions Ltd for their advertisement for INFO 84; Whittington Hospital for their job advertisements; Hugh Thomas, Hamish Hamilton Ltd and Harper & Row Ltd, Publishers, Inc. for an extract from *An Unfinished History of the World*, copyright © Hugh Thomas 1979; London Express News and Feature Services for 'Space test shatters scientists' by Erskine McCullough in *The Standard* (7.12.83.); an extract from *Play it Safe* reproduced by kind permission of the Health Education Council, London; Ford Motor Company Ltd for their car advertisement.

Copyright photographs are reproduced by courtesy of the following:

Sally and Richard Greenhill pp. 19 and 41; Rex Features p. 63; Barnaby's pp. 84 and 104.

Contents

Notes to the Student

Notes to the Student

The object of this book is to provide students preparing for the University of Cambridge First Certificate in English with complete practice in the Written and Oral papers. Each of the five tests consists of three written and two oral papers as follows:

WRITTEN PAPERS

Paper 1 Reading Comprehension (1 hour)

Section A Twenty-five multiple-choice questions testing vocabulary and formal grammatical control, in sentence contexts.

Section B Fifteen multiple-choice reading comprehension questions based on three or more texts, which may include information in graphic form, designed to test comprehension of gist or detailed content.

Paper 2 Composition (1½ hours)

Two compositions from a choice of descriptive, narrative or discursive topics, or topics based on prescribed reading.

Assessment will be based on organisation and clarity of content, accuracy of grammatical control, fluency and range of expression.

Paper 3 Use of English (2 hours)

Open-completion or transformation items designed to test active control of the language, followed by a directed writing exercise to test ability to interpret and present information.

ORAL PAPERS

Paper 4 Listening Comprehension (20 to 30 minutes)

Questions of varying type (selection, re-ordering, blank-filling, etc.) to test accurate understanding of spoken English, based on recorded material including conversation, announcements, etc.

Paper 5 Interview (12 to 15 minutes)

Based on a picture stimulus, and related passages and other material. The interview may, optionally, be based partly on one of the prescribed texts. It may be conducted, also optionally, with individual candidates or in groups of two or three. Assessment will be based on fluency and grammatical accuracy, pronunciation, communicative ability and vocabulary.

A Teacher's Edition of this book is available, with Answer Key, Marking Scheme and Tapescript.

Cassettes of the Listening Comprehension material for Paper 4 are available.

Test One

PAPER 1 READING COMPREHENSION (1 hour)

This paper is in two parts, section A and section B. For each question you answer correctly in section A you gain **one** *mark; for each question you answer correctly in section B you gain* **two** *marks. No marks are deducted for wrong answers. Answer all the questions. Indicate your choice of answer in every case on the separate answer sheet, which should show your name and examination index number. Follow carefully the instructions about how to record your answers.*

SECTION A

In this section you must choose the word or phrase which best completes each sentence. For each question, 1 to 25, indicate on your answer sheet the letter A, B, C or D against the number of the question.

1 The practice tests are reproduced in exactly the .... form as the examination.
   A similar   B same   C like   D equal

2 The giant slalom race was first .... in 1952.
   A founded   B induced   C commenced   D introduced

3 It took .... long time to solve the mystery.
   A too much   B a very   C ever so   D very much

4 Many Indians in North America live in tribal ....
   A enclosures   B compounds   C reservations   D reserves

5 Against his .... , Mario was forced to leave the country.
   A mind   B will   C instinct   D heart

6 The young people of today seem to believe in .... more than clothes and pop music.
   A not   B none   C nothing   D no

7 It has always .... me why you believe the Earth is flat.
   A muddled   B wondered   C puzzled   D confused

8 She idolised her son and practically raised him to the .... of a god.
   A grade   B prestige   C rank   D status

9 .... otherwise directed by a doctor, this medicine should be taken three times a day.
A Unless   B Except   C If   D Although

10 It took the soldier a long time to .... the death of his comrade.
A get round   B get over   C get across   D get through

11 If I .... sing as well as you, I'd be a millionaire.
A could   B would   C will   D should

12 After a week the bubbles .... down to a regular rate.
A steady   B sink   C stay   D settle

13 I never .... a chance of improving my English if I can help it.
A miss   B lose   C avoid   D waste

14 Would you .... a minute please, I'll try to connect you.
A keep on   B stay on   C hold on   D stop on

15 The XYZ Video .... contains details of over 300 productions.
A brochure   B leaflet   C prospectus   D catalogue

16 Saturday morning cinemas for children are, ... , a thing of the past.
A all in all   B on the whole   C in the long run   D bit by bit

17 Which would you .... have, the red or the blue one?
A better   B prefer   C rather   D choose

18 The doctor gave the woman a strong .... to calm her down.
A antidote   B sedative   C bromide   D antiseptic

19 Many people who go to see their bank managers have a .... problem.
A cash flow   B petty cash   C cash-book   D cashing up

20 Because of the increasing interest in horse riding, there is a growing need for
....
A goldsmiths   B locksmiths   C silversmiths   D blacksmiths

21 I have always posted my letters first class, ... it costs more.
A because   B although   C since   D while

22 Atlantis was a legendary island in the Atlantic Ocean first .... by Plato.
A referred   B informed   C mentioned   D quoted

23 He knew he must .... nothing of this to his wife.
    A breathe   B secrete   C talk   D discuss

24 The .... native American music is jazz, which was born in New Orleans.
    A one   B single   C alone   D only

25 .... is not allowed on double yellow lines.
    A A parking   B Parking   C Some parking   D Any parking

SECTION B

In this section you will find after each of the passages a number of questions or unfinished statements about the passage, each with four suggested answers or ways of finishing. You must choose the one which you think fits best. For each question, 26 to 40, indicate on your answer sheet the letter A, B, C or D against the number of the question.

FIRST PASSAGE

I had reached Port Said from Alexandria about an hour before, after 7.00 p.m. It is a long drive but a rewarding one, and when I told the driver not to hurry, it was not because of the wrecked cars at the side of the road. The delta of the Nile is a wide expanse of glimmering greenness, water, villages and animals. Everywhere men and women walk behind ploughs, or sit in groups under eucalyptus trees or the weeping willows that bow over scores of canals and small rivers – all the many waterways that make up the miracle that has nourished old Egypt since before the building of the pyramids. You drive through white-pink fields of cotton dotted with the larger blobs of pink, white, red and blue that are the robes, turbans and dresses of villagers working in the sun. Behind mud-coloured village walls, outlines of minarets rise from screens of palm trees. Men and boys wash naked in streams by the roadsides, the mud-thickened water modestly encircling them as they stand waist-high. One sees railway lines, factory chimneys and pylons carrying high-tension wires that connect the industrial towns of the delta with Alexandria or Cairo, but the great rich greenness flows away to the skyline, never interrupted for long. It is a landscape with moving figures of countless men and animals and a restless profusion of birds.

As evening fell, on the straight coast road between Damietta and Port Said, the taxi ran full tilt into a rock, shattering the front axle. The stone was difficult to see at dusk against the grey road. My driver waved down a passing car, and its owner drove us, crying, 'No problem, no problem. You do the same for me,' to the Holiday Hotel, the hotel recommended to me by Captain Roncallo. The taxi driver, who had friends who

3

owned a garage in Port Said, didn't seem worried about his front axle, and said goodbye in good spirits.

The hotel was quite modern. On a card in my room I read that television involved an additional charge but, when I turned it on, it showed nothing on seven of its eight channels and, on the eighth, a snowstorm from which came garbled American voices. After a shower I asked the receptionist if he would either remove the television charge from my bill or the set from my room.

He seemed astonished. 'But TV is compulsory,' he said.

'But there is no TV reception in Port Said.'

'You see here, sir, our card, it says – room service so-much, with breakfast compulsory so-much more. And then TV compulsory so-much more. And a fridge and radio and air-con, all so-much more. Tax extra, ten per cent.'

'Have you a room without TV, please?'

'Sir, all rooms have TV, fridge and radio. No one ever said before what you say about not wanting one.'

Another receptionist joined in. 'TV is like breakfast. Breakfast is compulsory. So is TV.'

'Yes, but breakfast is food – to eat, to live. TV actually doesn't exist here. Breakfast exists; you eat it!'

But there was no comprehension. It was written on the card, so I paid for the non-existent television.

26   The writer told the driver not to hurry because he wanted to

    A   reach Port Said in the evening.

    B   avoid becoming tired on the long journey.

    C   admire the changing scenery.

    D   avoid having a car accident.

27   What did the writer observe about the Nile delta?

    A   It was extremely fertile.

    B   It appeared overcrowded.

    C   The fields were divided by mud walls.

    D   The villages were built by the rivers.

28   Most of the people who lived in the delta were

    A   railway workers.

    B   agricultural labourers.

    C   farm owners.

    D   factory workers.

29 Why didn't the taxi driver worry about the accident?

    A   There was little damage done to the taxi.

    B   He quickly got a lift into Port Said.

    C   He could get the taxi repaired easily.

    D   The car driver offered to help him.

30 What made the writer become angry?

    A   The hotel wouldn't change his room.

    B   He could only receive one TV channel.

    C   The hotel staff were rude to him.

    D   He felt he was being cheated.

SECOND PASSAGE

It's often hard for those of us who have achieved the status of honoured parent to appreciate quite how spoilt the children of the 1980s are when it comes to TV and films. Anything less than total visual perfection and watch out for trouble as you shuffle out through the doorway marked 'EXIT'. But we must be firm occasionally, so next time your child observes that, personally, he would have expected a decaying body to have had a somewhat greener colour, seize him by the ear and remind him that when *you* were young, people used to run out of the cinema crying with terror as a cloth-covered rubber gorilla sat on top of a cardboard skyscraper and snatched balsawood aeroplanes out of the sky.

If any one man may be held responsible for this state of affairs then it must be Tony Dyson, creator of R2D2 in the film *The Empire Strikes Back*. If it were not for him, then film special effects would still be back in the far-off innocent days of jerky paper dinosaurs. Brian Johnson, who was in charge of the special effects of *The Empire Strikes Back*, ordered not just one, but eight editions of the robot which was soon to win the hearts of audiences the world over as R2D2. It took the Dyson workshop five months of frantic labour but the order was met in time for the start of the shooting of the film.

After the success of R2D2, other film and television work followed; a great deal for the Oxford Scientific Film series of wildlife documentaries. But Tony Dyson has always been an enthusiastic reader of science fiction, ever since childhood, and his old interest soon led him back to robots of one kind or another; and this time to robots for advertising purposes. Phil the android was designed for Philips domestic appliances and this two metre robot has appeared in children's TV programmes, in stores up and down the country, at exhibitions as well as in television commercials.

Tony has now completed work on Harry, an animated advertising cartoon with a difference in that he holds conversations with his audiences. But his main interest at the moment is the launching of Droid-Factory Ltd; a company set up specially to rent out promotional robots to marketing companies. So if a metallic-looking creature comes up to you next time you are in a supermarket and gives you an unasked for monologue on the virtues of such and such a washing powder, don't panic. The chances are that it's only one of Mr Dyson's employees. You should become alarmed only when it passes you by and strikes up a conversation with another of its own kind.

31 How are children nowadays different from their parents, according to the passage?

A They have perfect eyesight.

B They cause trouble in cinemas.

C They are more visually aware.

D They are more easy to spoil.

32   The writer suggests that parents should

    A   control their children by twisting their ears.

    B   stand no nonsense from their children.

    C   scare their children by taking them to horror films.

    D   encourage their children to see old films.

33   What is the importance of Tony Dyson to the cinema?

    A   He was the first man to produce special effects.

    B   He produced models of dinosaurs out of paper.

    C   He created the film *The Empire Strikes Back*.

    D   He changed people's expectations of special effects.

34   For the film *The Empire Strikes Back*

    A   several models of a robot were created.

    B   it took Dyson five months to make R2D2.

    C   Brian Johnson created R2D2 specially.

    D   there were eight different types of robot made.

35   Dyson invented Phil the android to

    A   be displayed in shops.

    B   make appearances on television.

    C   advertise a product.

    D   appear at exhibitions.

36   Nowadays Dyson is mainly interested in

    A   having conversations with robots.

    B   establishing a company.

    C   appearing in supermarkets.

    D   selling promotional robots.

THIRD PASSAGE

RATES EFFECTIVE 11th APRIL 1983		TIME PLUS MILEAGE			UNLIMITED MILEAGE (unlimited mileage rates will be charged on ALL rentals of 4 days or over.)		
GROUP	VEHICLE TYPE	Per day 1-3 days	Free miles	Excess Miles (per mile)	Per day 4-6 days	Per day 7-27 days	Per day 28 days and over
A	14 cwt Ford Escort	£11.75	50	9p	£16.25	£13.50	£12.50
B	1 ton Ford Transit	£13.50	50	10p	£18.50	£15.50	£14.00
D	35 cwt Ford Transit Dropside	£22.50	50	11p	£28.00	£23.00	£21.00
D	35 cwt Ford Transit Luton	£22.50	50	11p	£28.00	£23.00	£21.00
E	4 ton Ford Dropside	£34.00	50	12p	£40.00	£33.00	£30.00
E	4 ton Ford Box Van	£34.00	50	12p	£40.00	£33.00	£30.00

All rates are subject to VAT applicable at time of rental.
Additional hours are charged at 1/6 of the daily rate.

Short term contract rates can be specially negotiated for longer periods of rental. Call your local office for details.

Rental Information

Rates All rates include third party insurance, A.A. membership, maintenance and oil, but exclude fuel. Minimum period of rental is one day. Rates subject to change without notice.
Extension of Rental Should you wish to extend your rental beyond the agreed terminating date, it is most important that the renting depot is advised immediately and the required additional deposit paid so that insurance cover is extended. Failure to do so may mean that the renter is driving the vehicle without insurance.
Overseas Use Godfrey Davis Europcar commercial vehicles can be taken abroad at the daily time plus mileage rates quoted plus a surcharge of 20%. Unlimited mileage is not available on any rental which includes continental use. Additional insurance cover can be arranged on behalf of clients. (Rates available on request.)
Loss of or Damage to the Vehicle The renter is responsible for amount indicated below for each and every incident involving any damage to or loss of the vehicle during the rental period. Renter's liability may be waived by payment of collision damage waiver fee indicated. Payment of the premium reduces deposit to amount shown plus the estimated cost of rental.

		Group A + B	Group D	Group E
Renter responsible for first accidental damage or loss		£250.00	£300.00	£550.00
Collision damage waiver	per day	£2.50	£3.50	£5.50
	per week	£15.40	£22.75	£35.00
On payment of CDW deposit reduced	from	£250.00	£300.00	£550.00
	to	£20.00	£30.00	£40.00
		PLUS ESTIMATED COST OF RENTAL		

Renters under 25 years of age *must* purchase collision damage waiver.
Overhead Damage Payment of the collision damage waiver does not void the renter's responsibility for damage caused as a result of striking overhead objects.
Personal Accident Cover and Goods in Transit Insurance Please ask for separate leaflets giving details of additional insurance cover available.
Drivers Drivers must produce a current and suitable driving licence which has been held for at least one year. Unless the renter is providing comprehensive insurance cover, the driver must be between 21 and 70 years of age. No person other than the renter or approved driver is allowed to drive the vehicle.

All rentals are subject to the standards terms and conditions appearing on the Rental Agreement and supplemented as above.
1 mile = 1.609 kilometres.

37 How much would it cost per day to rent a Ford Transit Dropside for a fortnight?

A £33.00

B £22.50

C £23.00

D £28.00

38 A driver aged twenty wants to rent a vehicle. He hasn't got comprehensive insurance. Which vehicles would he be allowed to drive?

    A   Group A only.

    B   All groups.

    C   Groups A and B.

    D   None.

39 To reduce the amount payable on loss of a rented vehicle you should

    A   have a suitable driving licence.

    B   purchase a collision damage waiver.

    C   accept responsibility for the loss.

    D   take out additional insurance.

40 When driving a group D vehicle abroad for 3 days, you have to pay

    A   £22.50 per day + excess mileage + 20%.

    B   £28.00 per day + 11p each mile + 20%.

    C   £23.00 per day + 11p each mile.

    D   £22.50 per day + 20% on each mile over 50.

PAPER 2 COMPOSITION (1½ hours)

*Write **two only** of the following composition exercises. Your answers must follow exactly the instructions given, and must be of between 120 and 180 words each.*

1 Write a letter of complaint to the manufacturer about a defective domestic appliance that you have recently bought.

2 Persuade a friend to read a book that you have greatly enjoyed yourself.

3 Write an account of a recent exhibition that you have visited.

4 What are the advantages or disadvantages of computers?

5 (See Appendix : Prescribed texts)

PAPER 3   USE OF ENGLISH (2 hours)

SECTION A

1   *Fill each of the numbered blanks in the following passage. Use only **one** word in each space.*

Down below, the boy picked his .... (1) over piles of rubble to the blocked tunnel. .... (2) the roar of the rockfall, the caves seemed eerily quiet. The air was .... (3) with dust, and he kept his handkerchief pressed .... (4) over his mouth. With his free hand he .... (5) up a small stone and banged it on .... (6) of the huge rocks .... (7) filled the entrance to the tunnel. The clinking sound echoed .... (8) into the recesses of the cave system, and .... (9) the silence returned once .... (10), heavy with menace. The boy had the uneasy feeling that at .... (11) moment, the place .... (12) decide to bury him as well. He couldn't explain .... (13), he knew it was impossible, ... (14) he was suddenly convinced that .... (15) intricate mine network had a mind of its .... (16).

He banged on the rock again and called, 'Bill...?' His .... (17) ricocheted off the walls, and he .... (18) hear the hopelessness in it. Could there .... (19) be life behind that solid mass? The odds against it were long, and getting .... (20) with every passing minute.

2   *Finish each of the following sentences in such a way that it means exactly the same as the sentence printed before it.*

> EXAMPLE: I've never been to America before.
>
> ANSWER: This is *the first time that I have ever been to America.*

a)   Who is going on the trip tomorrow?

   How ....

b)   The regulations weren't changed until the students protested.

   By ....

c)   My son gets dirtier than all the other children.

   The other children ....

d)   If the weather had been better, I'd have gone skiing.

   The weather ....

e)   I asked her to give me an early morning call the next day.

   'Please ....

f)   I'm afraid I have to cancel this afternoon's meeting.

   I regret not ....

g)   In spite of the hostile reception, he carried on.

   Although ....

h)   Do you think you can manage alone?

   Is it ....

i)   The painters decorated our house last week.

   We ....

j)   How do I get to the Town Hall, please?

   Which ....

3   *In each of the following sentences is a blank with a word just before it. Fill each blank with a word that combines with the one given, making a new word that fits the sentence.*

> EXAMPLE: Please put out your cigarette. There's an *ash* .... over there.

> ANSWER: *ashtray*

a)   Fasten all your papers together with a *paper* ....

b)   She's not a very good *time* .... , she's always late.

c)   The head of the *house* .... always has to fill in official forms.

d)   They left at *day* .... and didn't stop to eat until noon.

e)   Be careful! Don't spill that coffee on my clean *table* ....

f)   That tall tower over there is a *land* .... in the countryside.

g)   You need another *book* .... now you've bought all those new books.

h)   The beam from the *light* .... warns ships of hidden rocks.

USE FORMS OF LEAVE

4   *Complete each of the following sentences with the appropriate form of LEAVE.*

> EXAMPLE: As soon as the guests *leave*, clean up the rooms.

a)   Would you mind .... the door open, please?

b)   If he .... earlier, he wouldn't get caught in the rush hour.

c)   .... it alone! It's too hot to eat yet.

d)   I'd like you .... your name and address.

e)   By .... then, she avoided an argument.

f)   The train at platform 4 .... at 10.00 p.m.

5 *Susan has found a defect in a sweater she has bought and has gone back to the shop to complain. Fill in the parts of the dialogue, shown as a) to e), which are blank.*

    Susan: I bought this sweater here last week and there's something wrong with it.

a) *Shop assistant:* What .... ?

    Susan: Well, it has a flaw in the pattern.

b) *Shop assistant:* Where .... ?

    Susan: It's here, on the right sleeve.

c) *Shop assistant:* ....

    Susan: Yes, there is. Look, here, near the shoulder, just at the top.

d) *Shop assistant:* Why .... ?

    Susan: Well, I was in a hurry, and I didn't think to check it for flaws. What are you going to do about it?

e) *Shop assistant:* Would .... ?

    Susan: Hmm, I think I'd rather have my money back.

SECTION B

6 *Read the information given below about the International Baccalaureate, and about the four students: Maria Braga, Carol White, Yoshi Suzuki and Ahmed Aziz. Decide which combination of subjects would be most suitable for each of them at Higher and Subsidiary levels and give your answers, with reasons, in the spaces provided. Each answer should be in about 50 words.*

The INTERNATIONAL BACCALAUREATE

The International Baccalaureate (IB)

THE IB PROGRAMME is a two-year pre-university course leading either to the IB Diploma or to separate subject certificates depending on the student's abilities and plans for further education.

The IB programme assumes that education at upper secondary level should encompass the development of all the powers of the mind through which one interprets, modifies and enjoys the environment. Every IB student is required to become proficient in language and mathematics, to become familiar with at least one subject that exemplifies the study of scientific enquiry and to develop an acquaintance with aesthetic and moral values.

THE IB EXAMINATION
GENERAL SCHEME

The IB Diploma is awarded for satisfactory performance in **six** subjects:–

1. Language A (first language, generally the student's native language) – this includes a study of World Literature in translation from at least two continents and two language areas.

2. Language B (second modern language, distinguished from Language A in not requiring the same depth and breadth of understanding of the cultural and historical contexts of language), or a second Language A.

3. Study of Man – one of the following options:–
history, geography, economics, philosophy, psychology, social anthropology, business studies.

4. Experimental Sciences – one of the following options:–
biology, chemistry, applied chemistry, physics, physical science, scientific studies.

5. Mathematics.

6. One of the following:–
art, music, classical language, a second language B, an additional option from 3 or 4, further mathematics, a special syllabus developed by the school.

Three of these six subjects must be offered at Higher Level and three at Subsidiary Level.

IB Sample Programmes

Higher	Subsidiary		Higher	Subsidiary
Mathematics	English A		French A	Mathematics
Physics	German B	OR	Arabic B	School-based
Chemistry	History		Economics	science
				Art

The International Baccalaureate Office (IBO)
INTERNATIONAL ORGANISATION

The International Baccalaureate Office (IBO), based in Geneva, with regional offices in Buenos Aires, London, New York and Southampton and representatives in Jamaica and Singapore, is a foundation under Swiss law governed by an International Council. IBO is a non-governmental organisation holding consultative status with UNESCO and financed by school/examination fees and by government grants.

M<small>ARIA</small> B<small>RAGA</small>:
– Brazilian
– aged 16
– good at languages
– interested in social sciences

C<small>AROL</small> W<small>HITE</small>:
– British
– aged 17
– has studied the classics
– wants to be a doctor

Y<small>OSHI</small> S<small>UZUKI</small>:
– Japanese
– aged 15
– keen on business
– finds languages difficult

A<small>HMED</small> A<small>ZIZ</small>:
– Egyptian
– aged 16
– interested in maths and science
– wants to go to university

In my opinion, Carol White ....

....

....

....

I think that Ahmed Aziz ....

....

....

....

From my point of view, Maria Braga ....

....

....

....

To my way of thinking, Yoshi Suzuki ....

....

....

....

PAPER 4 LISTENING COMPREHENSION (20 to 30 minutes)

FIRST PART

Tick (√) whether the following statements are true or false.

	True	*False*
1 The football match was held in England.		
2 The English fans travelled by train and boat.		
3 The English supporters started the trouble in the bars before the match.		
4 The French police used tear gas in the bars.		
5 The English fans threw beer cans at the police.		
6 Parts of the seats were used to fight with.		
7 The French won the match.		
8 Police cars were overturned.		
9 Two English football fans were stabbed.		
10 Twenty-five supporters were detained by the police.		
11 The fans caused a lot of damage on the boat going home.		
12 The mayor of Paris intends to stop football violence.		

SECOND PART

13 *You will hear a woman talking about a women's safety committee. Tick the items which you hear mentioned in connection with women's safety. The first one has been done for you.*

a	better training for jobs	
b	more phone boxes	✓
c	support for nuclear safety	
d	improved maternity grants	
e	hostels for women	
f	police accountability	
g	better maternity agreements	
h	more day nurseries for children	
i	classes for self-defence	
j	improved childcare facilities	
k	protection from sexual harassment	
l	security patrols on estates	
m	improved social services	
n	better housing	
o	improved street lighting	

THIRD PART

You will hear a recorded phone announcement giving details of programmes at the Palace Cinema. Look at the advertisement first and then fill in the information you hear.

THE TRAVELOGUE ON MEXICO

starts (14) ....

PALACE CINEMA

doors open (15) ....

SENIOR CITIZENS

reduced prices (16) ....

LAST COMPLETE PROGRAMME

starts (17) ....

BOX-OFFICE

opens (18) ....

UPPER FOYER

licensed bar and (19) ....

....

Rumble Fish bears all the hallmarks of a palpable cult success . . .

Mick Brown–THE SUNDAY TIMES MAGAZINE

FRANCIS FORD COPPOLA
P R E S E N T S

rumble FISH

NOW
Palace Cinema 638 0691
SEPARATE PROGRAMMES DAILY 1.25; 3.20; 5.20; 7.20; 9.25 p.m.

PAPER 5   INTERVIEW (12 to 15 minutes)

SECTION A: PICTURE CONVERSATION

Look at this picture carefully and be prepared to answer some questions about it.

(See Teacher's Edition for suggested questions and topics.)

SECTION B: READING PASSAGE

Look at this passage and be prepared to answer some questions about it and then to read it aloud.

Hello...Peter? Good, now listen, I've finally managed to get some tickets for the concert. Yes, I know, I had to queue up for ages. Anyway it starts at 8.00, so can you meet me in the foyer about 7.30? I'd like to have time for a drink before it starts. Is that OK? Right, I'll see you there – and don't be late.

(See Teacher's Edition for suggested questions.)

SECTION C: STRUCTURED COMMUNICATION ACTIVITY

There may be a variety of options offered in this section. Choose one of the following:

a) You want to get to the airport but you are not sure which is the best way to go. Ask someone if they can help you.

    Find out: which is the best route to take.
                   how long it will take to get there.
                   how much it will cost approximately.

    Explain: which plane you have to catch.
                  what time it is leaving.
                  that you have a limited amount of money.

b) Group or pair work.

Look at these pictures, A, B and C, and find out which one contains all the pieces necessary to make the cowboy. Discuss the pictures with other members in your group.

c) (See Appendix: Prescribed texts)

Test Two

PAPER 1 READING COMPREHENSION (1 hour)

*This paper is in two parts, section A and section B. For each question you answer correctly in section A you gain **one** mark; for each question you answer correctly in section B you gain **two** marks. No marks are deducted for wrong answers. Answer all the questions. Indicate your choice of answer in every case on the separate answer sheet, which should show your name and examination index number. Follow carefully the instructions about how to record your answers.*

SECTION A

In this section you must choose the word or phrase which best completes each sentence. For each question, 1 to 25, indicate on your answer sheet the letter A, B, C or D against the number of the question.

1 She couldn't go out because she had a .... cold.
   A running   B flowing   C streaming   D leaking

2 Those children have very good table ....
   A conduct   B manners   C behaviour   D attitude

3 They serve .... refreshments on the train.
   A light   B little   C small   D slight

4 You can rely on him to .... your instructions.
   A carry off   B take out   C bring off   D carry out

5 We're going on a day .... to the island tomorrow.
   A visit   B voyage   C trip   D journey

6 Are the students .... about the examination?
   A talking   B discussing   C saying   D telling

7 Who do I make the cheque .... to?
   A in   B out   C up   D on

8 I have posted my application .... for a driving licence.
   A register   B form   C paper   D certificate

9 I tried to ring Mr Brown but his number was ....
   A occupied   B used   C employed   D engaged

10 What .... shoes do you take?
    A length   B measure   C size   D scale

11 The article was .... the front page of the newspaper.
    A on   B at   C in   D of

12 Do you .... to a lot of pop music?
    A attend   B hear   C listen   D overhear

13 I'm .... to go to America next summer.
    A decided   B agreed   C determined   D arranged

14 We must ask the plumber to repair that .... tap.
    A dribbling   B dripping   C dropping   D drooping

15 The injured man was taken to hospital .... ambulance.
    A with   B in   C by   D on

16 The price of package holidays has .... considerably this year.
    A declined   B lessened   C decreased   D fallen

17 He was out of .... after jogging round the park.
    A oxygen   B air   C breath   D wind

18 Be careful, because that knife is very ....
    A sharp   B blunt   C hard   D acute

19 I asked my teacher's .... about going to university.
    A information   B experience   C advice   D knowledge

20 I'll .... in my car on the way to work.
    A take you out   B bring you up   C let you off   D pick you up

21 He knows all Shakespeare's sonnets by ....
    A heart   B head   C mind   D memory

22 I can't remember .... the letter yesterday.
    A post   B posting   C posted   D to post

23 It was very cold .... they still went swimming.
    A although   B in spite of   C but   D though

24 They don't .... students run in the corridors.
    A allow   B permit   C accept   D let

25 Peter .... the company for his father.
    A runs   B works   C makes   D does

SECTION B

In this section you will find after each of the passages a number of questions or unfinished statements about the passage, each with four suggested answers or ways of finishing. You must choose the one which you think fits best. For each question, 26 to 40, indicate on your answer sheet the letter A, B, C or D against the number of the question.

FIRST PASSAGE

No meeting was attended by more controversy beforehand than the Mexico Games. The major problem was the high altitude of Mexico City—over 2,134 m. above sea-level—which meant that no middle- or long-distance runner from a low-altitude country had any real chance of beating the 'men of the mountains'. Australia's Ron Clarke, for example, went to Mexico as a multiple record-breaker but came close to collapse during the final stages of the 10,000 metres and had to be revived afterwards with an oxygen mask.

On the other hand, the thin air was an advantage in events like the short sprints and hurdles and the long and triple jumps.

It would be ungenerous, however, to deny the success of the African athletes in Mexico even though many of them had benefited from having lived or trained at high altitude. Kipchoge Keino of Kenya, for example, ran in the 10,000, 5,000 and 1,500 metres and his winning time of 3 min. 34·9 sec. in the 1,500 metres was without doubt effectively better than the then world record, set at low altitude, of 3 min. 33·1 sec.

But the choice of Mexico City for the 1968 games meant that, to give themselves a fair chance, many of the athletes had to sacrifice even more of their time to allow for special high-altitude training. One could no longer, it seemed, afford to be a part-timer in sport.

26 This passage is about

    A a race meeting.

    B playing games.

    C an international event.

    D a match.

27 The problem that faced some of the contestants was the

    A mountainous area.

    B depth of the sea.

    C remoteness of the area.

    D height of the location.

28 In which of these events were the climatic conditions a disadvantage?

    A   10,000 metres.

    B   Long jump.

    C   100 metres.

    D   Hurdles.

29 In the 1,500 metres, Kipchoge Keino's time

    A   was inside the world record.

    B   equalled the world record at 3 min. 33·1 sec.

    C   was outside the world record by less than two seconds.

    D   outdid the world record by 1·8 seconds.

30 Owing to the location, some athletes were obliged to

    A   train part time.

    B   change their routine.

    C   provide specialist training.

    D   give up some training time.

SECOND PASSAGE

1

RUDY RHODES, five times World Singles tennis champion, was sent off court yesterday for using foul language and throwing his racket at the spectators. He maintained that three double faults had been incorrectly called against him when serving for the match. The umpire, however, stood firm. After reminding Rhodes that he had already been warned several times for insulting behaviour on court, he disqualified him from competing further in the tournament.

2

Christine Hart, 22, a London primary school teacher, is so tired of being mistaken for TV star Lorna Loraine that she has dyed her blonde hair black and taken to wearing dark glasses.

'My boyfriend doesn't like it,' she told our reporter, 'but I had to do something. It's bad enough being pestered for your autograph every time you go into the supermarket, but it doesn't stop there. People ask all sorts of embarrassing questions about my private life and they simply won't believe me when I say I've never even spoken to Lorna Loraine.'

3

Dear Young Worried,
From what you say in your letter, I think you are being over-sensitive about your skin problem. Teenagers frequently suffer from spots at one time or another, but the trouble usually clears up with the right diet and regular application of a good cleansing cream. Make sure you eat plenty of fresh fruit and vegetables and drink lots of pure fruit juice. Cut out the cream buns and fizzy drinks. Take as much exercise in the open air as you can – jogging, swimming and tennis are all good. Remember to clean your face thoroughly every night. I recommend Goodheary's cleansing milk – available at any chemist, price £1.45.

4

A man charged with stealing £25,000 worth of jewellery from the home of millionairess, Mrs Betty Farlow, created a sensation in court yesterday when he claimed that all the jewellery was fake. To prove his point, he produced a pearl necklace which he alleged belonged to Mrs Farlow, broke the string and scattered the pearls all over the courtroom floor. The case was adjourned while court officials got down on their hands and knees to search for the pearls.

31 You would expect to find these items in a

A   sports magazine.

B   popular daily.

C   law report.

D   women's magazine.

32 Which headline appeared above item 2?

A   SPOT THE DIFFERENCE

B   CHAMPION MEETS HIS MATCH

C   FACE THE WORLD

D   SENSATION IN COURT

33 Item 1 refers to

A   criminal charges.

B   beauty care.

C   unsocial behaviour.

D   facial characteristics.

34 The letter contains

A   a warning.

B   advice.

C   an explanation.

D   an apology.

THIRD PASSAGE

British airways

Arriving at London Heathrow Airport

How to get into central London

Heathrow Airport is approximately 15 miles west of central London.

Bus
Convenient and inexpensive services operate from Terminals 1, 2 and 3 to points in central London.
Last bus: 21.55.   First bus: 03.35   Daily.

Underground railway
Heathrow is linked by the Piccadilly Line to the London Underground system.
Comparatively quick, but not recommended for passengers with large amounts of baggage.
Last train: 23.50.   First train: 05.07 (Weekdays), 06.48 (Sundays).

Taxi
Ranks for authorised (black) cabs are outside each terminal. Journeys of less than 20 miles in the London area must be charged according to the meter – otherwise agree the fare before the journey. If in doubt, consult a policeman or traffic warden. Do not use unlicensed cabs which are touted inside the terminal buildings.

Rail/Hotel/Car hire
British Rail, Hotel Bookings International and the major car hire companies all maintain information and reservation desks in the terminal buildings.

Transferring flights

The baggage claim check attached to your ticket shows the destination airport of your baggage. The letters LHR or LON mean it has been labelled only to London and MUST be claimed there and re-registered for your next flight.

International-to-International and Domestic-to-International
If your baggage has been labelled to your final destination, follow the yellow overhead 'Transfers'

Transfers ▲

signs to the British Airways Transfer Desk for check-in information. If your baggage has been labelled for London only, follow the 'Arrivals' signs to claim it before proceeding.

International-to-Domestic
If you are transferring to a flight to a destination in the UK follow the yellow overhead signs to 'Arrivals'.

Arrivals ▲

After completing immigration formalities you must claim your checked baggage, wherever it is labelled to, and clear Customs – or your baggage will remain in London. Then proceed with your baggage to Domestic Departures, Terminal 1.

Transfer buses
Yellow transfer buses run continuously between the terminal buildings. This service is free.

Transfers to Gatwick Airport
Heathrow and Gatwick are linked by ten helicopter flights a day. Flight time is approximately 15 minutes.

For check-in,
follow this sign:

There are also half-hourly Green Line bus services, the 727 taking 1 hour 40 minutes, and the non-stop 747 Jetlink 1 hour 10 minutes. In all cases your baggage must be cleared through Customs and taken with you.

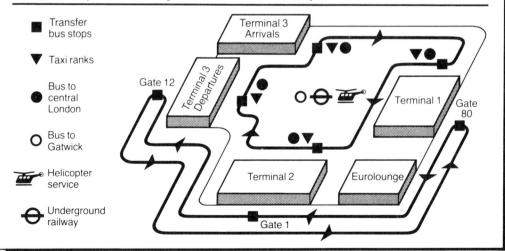

- ■ Transfer bus stops
- ▼ Taxi ranks
- ● Bus to central London
- ○ Bus to Gatwick
- Helicopter service
- Underground railway

35 The first public transport service operating from Heathrow to central London after 2.30 a.m. on Sundays is

A the London Underground.

B the Green Line service.

C British Airways.

D the bus service.

36 If you take a taxi from Heathrow for a distance of less than 20 miles

A the cost has to be agreed with the driver.

B you are charged at a standard rate.

C an official fixes the charge.

D you must obtain a licence.

37 Passengers transferring to another plane, whose baggage is marked LHR or LON, should first

A go to the British Airways transfer desk.

B have it re-labelled at Arrivals.

C claim it before checking-in.

D take it to Arrivals for checking.

38 Instructions are given for passengers leaving from Terminal 1 who are

A making internal flights.

B transferring to Gatwick Airport.

C travelling for domestic reasons.

D holders of British passports.

39 It is possible to get public transport from Heathrow to Gatwick

A at quarter-hour intervals.

B hourly.

C every thirty minutes.

D on the hour.

40 Which of these forms of transport at Heathrow makes no charge?

A The 747 Jetlink.

B The internal service.

C The 727 Green Line.

D The Piccadilly Line.

PAPER 2   COMPOSITION (1½ hours)

Write **two only** *of the following composition exercises. Your answers must follow exactly the instructions given, and must be of between 120 and 180 words each.*

1   You are taking an important examination in two months' time. You have had an accident and are in hospital with a broken leg. Write a letter to your teacher explaining what has happened and asking if you can have some work sent to you to continue your studies while you are in hospital.

2   You want your friend to meet your eleven-year-old nephew at the airport while you are at work. Tell him/her when and where your nephew will be arriving, how to identify him and where to take him to wait for you.

3   Describe a radio or TV programme you particularly enjoy. Give your reasons.

4   Are friends more important than money?

5   (See Appendix : Prescribed texts)

PAPER 3 USE OF ENGLISH (2 hours)

SECTION A

1 *Fill each of the numbered blanks in the following passage. Use only* **one** *word in each space.*

According to a newspaper .... (1) yesterday, a man is .... (2) to have drowned .... (3) jumping into the Thames .... (4) Westminster Bridge at the end of a high-speed police car .... (5). It seems that the trouble .... (6) when the man failed to .... (7) when signalled to .... (8) the police. A police launch immediately set out .... (9) Waterloo Bridge to try to .... (10) him but he .... (11) not be found. A policeman said that they pursued the man round Whitehall but he .... (12) to escape them and drove straight to Westminster Bridge .... (13) he .... (14) in. The police have issued a description, but so .... (15) no one has reported him .... (16). He was apparently in his .... (17) thirties and was .... (18) a light brown, casual .... (19) and a red woollen hat. He was driving a Mini Metro, ... (20) number A526 KLM.

2 *Finish each of the following sentences in such a way that it means exactly the same as the sentence printed before it.*

      EXAMPLE: I don't go to the cinema very often.

      ANSWER: I seldom *go to the cinema.*

a)   She said she was sorry she hadn't finished her homework.

      She apologised ....

b)   He left college four years ago.

      It ....

c)   'Can you lend me five pounds, John?' said Mary.

      Mary asked ....

d)   The hotel was fully booked.

      There ....

e)   It's no use waiting any longer for the bus.

      There's no ....

f)   It isn't necessary for you to go to all that trouble.

      You ....

g)   Have you used all the coffee?

      Isn't ....

h)   I haven't smoked for two years now.

      I gave ....

i)   What is your father's profession?

      What does ....

j)   I like swimming.

      I'm ....

3 *Complete the following sentences with the correct preposition or particle.*

   EXAMPLE: Sales have fallen *off* .... this year.

   a) He fell .... the stairs.

   b) My birthday falls .... a Monday this year.

   c) Be careful the baby doesn't fall .... of that chair.

   d) Their holiday plans have fallen ....

   e) The child fell .... in the playground.

4 *Substitute a word or phrase with the same meaning for* hard *in the following sentences.*

   EXAMPLE: This bed is very hard.

   ANSWER: This bed is *very uncomfortable* .

   a) The examination was very hard.

   ....

   b) I'm afraid we're going to have a hard winter.

   ....

   c) Losing his job was very hard luck.

   ....

   d) The bread was so hard I couldn't eat it.

   ....

   e) My stepmother was a very hard woman.

   ....

5 *Make all the changes and additions necessary to produce, from the following eight sets of words and phrases, eight sentences which together make a complete letter. Note carefully from the example what kind of alterations need to be made. Write each sentence in the space provided.*

EXAMPLE: I/sorry/not able/meet you/before now.

ANSWER: *I'm sorry I have not been able to meet you before now.*

Dear Member of Staff,

As you know I/recently/appoint/Welfare Officer/this factory.

a) ....

That/mean/I/be responsible for/make/sure/you/be/all/happy/your work.

b) ....

I/send/this letter/everyone and I/hope/that in time/I/get/know/you all personally.

c) ....

It/be/very important/you/feel/able/come/me/with any problem/that/trouble/you/however trivial/it/seem.

d) ....

I/not want/you/think/of me/as/just/a name on a door.

e) ....

My office hours/be/from 9.30 a.m. – 5.30 p.m. but you/not have/make/an appointment.

f) ....

If I/be/not/my office/leave/message with my secretary.

g)   ....

I/get/in touch/you/soon/possible.

h)   ....

Yours sincerely,

Martha Haggard

Welfare Officer

SECTION B

6   *Using only the information contained in the extract below, write three paragraphs continuing the conversation between Gerry and Alan. You will probably need about 50 words for each paragraph.*

How shall I find the way?

Signposts. Many public paths are signposted where they leave the metalled road; some, but not many, are also waymarked with painted arrows at tricky points. But few footpath signposts tell you where the path goes and far too often the route is obstructed or even obliterated by farmers. So you need maps.

Maps. Britain is one of the best-mapped countries in the world. The Ordnance Survey, the official survey and mapping agency, covers the whole country with maps of various scales. For walkers the best are the Landranger series at 1:50,000 (about one and a quarter inches to the mile) and the Pathfinder and Outdoor Leisure series at 1:25,000 (about two and a half inches to the mile). The bigger scale of course give you more detail (field boundaries especially) but you can quickly run out of map. The Landrangers won't help you when you need to know which side of the fence the right of way is, but they will see you through most walking and give you a good overview of a decent chunk of country. All these sheets mark rights of way, but the Pathfinder and Leisure ones do not yet cover the whole country.

Guidebooks make handy supplements to the maps. There are hundreds of them written just for walkers by local enthusiasts who have picked the best walks and the clearest paths. Often these books have handy sketch-maps and they tell you what to see or look out for along the way. They also grade the walks by distance so that you can pick an easy stroll for the family with small children or something longer and more demanding. The Ramblers' Association's fact sheets list guidebooks county by county.

Gerry: Maureen and I are taking the kids on a walking holiday this year. We've joined the Ramblers' Association, of course, but I'm a bit worried in case we get lost. I suppose all the paths are signposted?

Alan: ....

....

....

....

....

Gerry: What sort of map do you think I ought to take?

Alan: ....

....

....

....

....

Gerry: I want to get a good guidebook, but I'm not sure which is the best. I don't want the children to miss anything really interesting but, on the other hand, they're only eight and eleven and I don't want to tire them out.

Alan: ....

....

....

....

....

PAPER 4   LISTENING COMPREHENSION (20 to 30 minutes)

FIRST PART

1   *Listen to the conversation between Linda and Carol and complete the form by filling in the information you hear.*

MONEY-BACK SATISFACTION. All orders will be acknowledged. Allow up to 28 days delivery, and rest assured that if you are not completely happy with your choice and return garment unworn within 7 days, the Stephen House guarantee promises you a full refund.

STEPHEN HOUSE

KNOTTINGLEY, YORKSHIRE

To: Stephen House, Chapel Street, Knottingley, Yorkshire WF11 9AW.

Please send me _____ Wool/Cashmere suit(s) at £49.95 (plus £1.95 p&p) each.

Please send me _____ Silk shirt(s) at £9.95 each (post-free). I enclose my cheque/postal order for £ _____ made payable to Readers' Account, Stephen House, or debit my American Express/Diners/Access

card no. _____

Signature ___ L . Bolton _____

Name (Print) ___ LINDA BOLTON _____

Address _____

_____ Postcode _____

SIZE	10	12	14	16	18	20
SUIT Cool Grey						
SHIRT Black						
SHIRT White						

Remittances should be made payable to Readers' Account, Stephen House and shall be held on your behalf in this account until the goods are despatched. Reg. Office, Stephen House, Chapel Street, Knottingley, Yorkshire WF11 9AW. Reg. No. 1131560.
Orders from G.B., Channels., N. Ireland and BFPO welcome.   SEM29/1

Made entirely in the U.K.

SECOND PART

For questions 2–4 put a tick (√) in one of the boxes A, B, C or D.

2   This demonstration is taking place at

A   a cookery class.

B   an electrical shop.

C   a department store.

D   a House and Home exhibition.

A
B
C
D

3   One of the chief advantages of the Golden Glow toaster is that it is

    A   self-cleaning.

    B   economical.

    C   time-wasting.

    D   automatic.

A
B
C
D

4   What are you advised to do before using a new toaster?

    A   Wait eight minutes.

    B   Grease the inside.

    C   Pour oil on it.

    D   Keep it closed.

A
B
C
D

For question 5 number the instructions for using the toaster in the correct order 1–8. Put the number in the box. The first one has been done for you.

5

a	Check that the red light has gone off.	
b	Butter the bread and fill the sandwiches.	
c	Plug it in.	1
d	Close the lid and switch on.	
e	Re-close the lid.	
f	Remove sandwiches from toaster.	
g	Put sandwiches in toaster.	
h	Wait two minutes.	

For question 6 tick (√) the boxes for the answers you choose.

6   Which of these things are you advised *never* to do when using a Golden Glow toaster?

a	Switch off to clean.	
b	Bang the lid down.	
c	Keep it on for more than two minutes.	
d	Immerse it in water.	
e	Butter the bread inside.	
f	Cut the bread with a sharp knife.	
g	Allow cheese filling to melt.	
h	Clean with abrasives.	

THIRD PART

Look at the map and then tick whether the following statements are true or false.

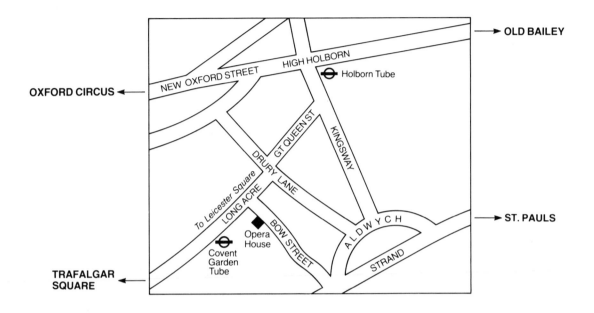

	True	False

7 A traffic warden is making this announcement.

8 An accident has occurred in Holborn tube station.

9 Six people have been killed.

10 A vehicle went out of control.

11 The area has been sealed off.

12 Rescue services were on the scene in minutes.

13 All roads between the Strand and New Oxford Street have been closed to traffic.

14 The lorry was carrying inflammable liquid.

15 All traffic has been diverted to High Holborn.

16 Public transport has been disrupted.

FOURTH PART

For each of the questions 17–20 put a tick (√) in one of the boxes, A, B, C or D.

17 This announcement is intended for people

    A   boarding a plane.

    B   meeting arrivals.

    C   checking in.

    D   arriving late.

A
B
C
D

18 The delay is due to

    A   high winds.

    B   poor visibility.

    C   thunderstorms.

    D   wintry conditions.

A
B
C
D

19 The plane is expected to arrive at

    A   a quarter to four.

    B   four fifteen.

    C   ten to five.

    D   five past four.

A
B
C
D

20 Enquiries should be made to

    A   a travel agent.

    B   a booking clerk.

    C   an airline representative.

    D   an airport official.

A
B
C
D

PAPER 5   INTERVIEW (12 to 15 minutes)

SECTION A: PICTURE CONVERSATION

Look at this picture carefully and be prepared to answer some questions about it.

(See Teacher's Edition for suggested questions and topics.)

SECTION B: READING PASSAGE

Look at this passage and be prepared to answer some questions about it and then to read it aloud.

Londoners may be able to travel on one ticket with British Rail included in the booming Travelcard system. The Travelcard, which is currently valid on London Transport's buses and tubes, has opened up unimagined opportunities. Sales have generated £25 million more than expected. If rail travel were included, Londoners could then choose the route they preferred.

(See Teacher's Edition for suggested questions.)

SECTION C: STRUCTURED COMMUNICATION ACTIVITY

There may be a variety of options offered in this section. Choose one of the following:

a) You are a teacher. A student left a diary in your classroom and it has gone.

   Ask the student: where and when he/she left it.
                     what it was like and what it contained.

   Advise: reporting the loss to the school secretary.

b) Group or pair work.

   Mr and Mrs Jones and their two children, 8 and 11, are planning to move out of London to a new town. Which of these facilities do you think are important?
      1   good schools
      2   frequent public transport
      3   shopping centre
      4   cinemas and theatres
      5   sports amenities
      6   hospital and medical care
      7   night life
      8   clean air
      9   pleasant neighbours
      10 low crime rate

c) (See Appendix: Prescribed texts)

Test Three

PAPER 1   READING COMPREHENSION (1 hour)

This paper is in two parts, section A and section B. For each question you answer correctly in section A you gain **one** *mark; for each question you answer correctly in section B you gain* **two** *marks. No marks are deducted for wrong answers. Answer all the questions. Indicate your choice of answer in every case on the separate answer sheet, which should show your name and examination index number. Follow carefully the instructions about how to record your answers.*

SECTION A

In this section you must choose the word or phrase which best completes each sentence. For each question, 1 to 25, indicate on your answer sheet *the letter A, B, C or D against the number of the question.*

1   Although Lucy was slimming, she found cream cakes quite ....
    A imperative   B inevitable   C irresistible   D irrepressible

2   I like going to the zoo; ...., I want to see the baby seals.
    A besides   B further   C including   D likewise

3   He had worked with wood all his life and was a skilled ....
    A potter   B carpenter   C thatcher   D plumber

4   You should pay .... within twenty-five days of receiving your statement.
    A for good   B as a whole   C all told   D in full

5   Hot meals available here. Drop in for a .... to eat.
    A bite   B sip   C bit   D nip

6   Thomas .... with the other students at the bridge.
    A outdistanced   B gained   C caught up   D overtook

7   By the time the train arrived I was .... late.
    A eventually   B already   C therefore   D soon

8   The middle-aged couple had been attacked by muggers and were badly ....
    A smashed up   B beaten up   C softened up   D broken up

9   The ancient Egyptians believed all illnesses were related to .... was eaten.
    A which   B how   C what   D when

43

10 .... , the ship's crew consisted of forty-one men.
   A Entirely   B Completely   C Wholly   D Altogether

11 The members look forward to .... you to the committee.
   A joining   B welcoming   C entering   D meeting

12 On a sudden .... , she bought a ticket back home.
   A keenness   B feeling   C resolve   D impulse

13 When I give the .... I want you to start; so ready, steady, go!
   A warning   B signal   C gun   D shout

14 The heavy traffic .... over the bridge.
   A droned   B boomed   C rumbled   D drummed

15 I stared hard and .... just about see the airport in the distance.
   A was able   B should   C can   D could

16 Sanskrit is the .... member of the Indo-European family of languages.
   A eldest   B aged   C oldest   D ancient

17 Try our delicious three-course meal, offering you superb .... for money.
   A value   B worth   C cost   D price

18 I won't go to the party .... you come too.
   A except   B although   C until   D unless

19 The general .... orders to shoot the prisoners.
   A commanded   B issued   C notified   D declared

20 The marriage will .... next Monday at noon.
   A take place   B go off   C come together   D carry on

21 Why don't you sit .... me?
   A next   B along   C beside   D close

22 The soldier had to .... for disobeying orders.
   A stand trial   B serve notice   C hear sentence   D prove innocent

23 The snow has been .... steadily for several hours and the ground is
   completely covered.
   A flowing   B dropping   C drifting   D falling

24 Not .... has been arranged yet. You will have to wait.
   A something   B nothing   C everything   D anything

25 The colours were beautiful when the sun set .... the sea.
   A on   B over   C above   D by

SECTION B

In this section you will find after each of the passages a number of questions or unfinished statements about the passage, each with four suggested answers or ways of finishing. You must choose the one which you think fits best. For each question, 26 to 40, indicate on your answer sheet the letter A, B, C or D against the number of the question.

FIRST PASSAGE

When Laura approached school-going age the discussions about moving became more urgent. Her father did not want the children to go to school with the hamlet children and for once her mother agreed with him. Not because, as he said, they ought to have a better education than they could get at Lark Rise; but because she feared they would tear their clothes and catch cold and get dirty heads going the mile and a half to and from the school in the village. So vacant cottages in the market town were inspected and often it seemed that the next week or the next month they would be leaving Lark Rise for ever; but, again, each time something would happen to prevent the removal, and, gradually, a new idea arose. To gain time, their father would teach the two eldest children to read and write, so that, if approached by the School Attendance Office, their mother could say they were leaving the hamlet shortly and, in the meantime, were being taught at home.

So their father brought home two copies of Mavor's First Reader and taught them the alphabet; but just as Laura was beginning on words of one syllable, he was sent away to work on a distant job, only coming home at week-ends. Laura, left at the 'C-a-t s-i-t-s on the m-a-t' stage, had then to carry her book round after her mother as she went about her housework, asking: 'Please, Mother, what does h-o-u-s-e spell?' or 'W-a-l-k, Mother, what is that?' Often when her mother was too busy or too irritated to attend to her, she would sit and gaze on a page that might as well have been printed in Hebrew for all she could make of it, frowning and poring over the print as though she would wring out the meaning by force of concentration.

After weeks of this, there came a day when, quite suddenly, as it seemed to her, the printed characters took on a meaning. There were still many words, even in the first pages of that simple primer, she could not decipher; but she could skip those and yet make sense of the whole. 'I'm reading! I'm reading!' she cried aloud. 'Oh, Mother! Oh, Edmund! I'm reading!'

26 Laura's father didn't want his children to go to school at Lark Rise because

    A   it was too far away.

    B   they would ruin their clothes.

    C   their hair would become infested.

    D   they wouldn't learn enough.

27 Why didn't Laura's family leave Lark Rise?

    A   They were unable to find other suitable accommodation.

    B   They couldn't make up their minds where to live.

    C   Unexpected circumstances prevented them from doing so.

    D   They kept having new ideas about moving.

28 The children's father decided to teach them to read and write so that they

    A   could write to the School Attendance Board.

    B   had an excuse not to have to move.

    C   would be educated before they left the hamlet.

    D   had a reason for not attending school.

29 Initially Laura found it difficult to learn to read because

    A   her father was frequently away.

    B   nobody would answer her questions.

    C   her mother was uninterested in her.

    D   she only understood words of one syllable.

30 What made Laura gaze intently at a page in her book?

    A   Her inability to comprehend.

    B   Her lack of concentration.

    C   Her need to understand Hebrew.

    D   Her determination to understand.

31 Laura finally discovered she could read when she

    A   understood all the words in her book.

    B   recognised the printed characters.

    C   grasped the general meaning.

    D   skipped the first pages of her primer.

SECOND PASSAGE

Los Angeles cabinet-maker Edward Stewart may be a modern Dr Frankenstein. In 1959, he claims, he restored a dead friend to life with a simple technique. He opened the dead man's chest, rubbed his heart with a 'secret, life-giving' plant juice, then stimulated the heartbeat with 110 volts of electricity. The friend, says Stewart, has been living in Hawaii ever since.

Stewart also claims his revivification technique works on the small animals he suffocates in jars in his garage. It takes three hours to revive a dead mouse, he reports, and five hours for a small dog. 'Sometimes,' he adds, 'I buy those little chicken hearts in the supermarket, and I make them beat again using my plant juice before I cook them for dinner.'

According to Stewart, he discovered the plant juice one day while cutting hedges around his former home in Hawaii. Juice from one of the plants splattered onto his wrist, he says, and he suddenly noticed the skin begin to twitch. Nonetheless, he adds, he can't reveal the name of the plant. 'When the juice is zapped with electricity,' he says, 'it gives off a deadly gas.'

To promote his idea, Stewart has spent the past decade sending his papers to the University of California, the Army, and a number of government agencies. One scientist who evaluated the concept was Lynn Eldridge, of the Jerry Lewis Neuromuscular Research Center, in Los Angeles. She says Stewart may not be joking. 'The extracts from plants like belladonna are used to supply nutrients to human organs, which must be kept alive while travelling to a transplant. So Stewart might cut the heart out of a mouse and keep it alive with plant juice. But this effect is short-lived, and the organ must be placed into a healthy body or it dies. It's impossible to place a live organ in a dead body and expect it to revive every other organ in that body. I think Stewart has observed a basic scientific phenomenon, but his interpretation is crazy.'

Stewart recently discovered he had a cancerous growth. Though he admits he could leave instructions for someone to revive him should he die, he still goes for radiation treatment.

'If something went wrong with the plant juice,' he says, 'I wouldn't be around to perfect it and give it to mankind. Besides', he claims, 'government investigators are watching my garage. They've told me not to experiment on humans, which is a real shame.'

32 From the passage it would appear that Edward Stewart was
    A   a trained surgeon.
    B   an expert botanist.
    C   a skilled electrician.
    D   an experienced craftsman.

33 Stewart found certain plant juices were useful in his experiments when he
    A   noticed their effect on his skin.
    B   saw they contained electricity.
    C   realised they gave off gas fumes.
    D   discovered their secret names.

34 Why did Stewart send his research to various agencies?
    A   He wanted to become a university professor.
    B   He hoped the Army could use it in military warfare.
    C   He sought to get official recognition and acceptance.
    D   He hoped the government would invest money in the project.

35 Lynn Eldridge thinks there may be some truth in what Stewart says because
    A   organs containing plant extracts remain healthy indefinitely.
    B   dead bodies can be kept alive with transplanted organs.
    C   organs treated with certain plant juices revive dead bodies.
    D   extracts from certain plants help keep organs alive.

36 Why did Stewart decide to have treatment for his cancer?
    A   He didn't trust anyone to revive him if he died.
    B   He wanted to stay alive to continue his human experiments.
    C   He was afraid something might happen to the plant extracts.
    D   He thought it was his duty to test the treatment for mankind.

THIRD PASSAGE

Languages Library

Subjects and arrangement
Lending stock

The Library is arranged by language, each having its own 'area studies' section.

Languages not included in the B.A. syllabus are placed alphabetically in the Minor Languages section, and shelving is in classification number order, with dictionaries at the beginning of each sequence, and journals in boxes at the end.

The B.A. languages (Arabic, Chinese, French, German, Italian, Russian, Spanish) and English follow in larger individual sections where the books on politics, economics, history etc. are shelved in classification number order, but literary and critical works relating to specific authors are shelved in alphabetical order of author, regardless of class number. Dictionaries in these languages are shelved separately, except for Chinese and Arabic, where they precede the ordinary stock.

The General section includes books which do not confine their coverage to a single geographical area, and most books on linguistics.

Reference books

Books marked REF are for use in the Library only. Some of these are integrated on the shelves with the lending stock, but the following are shelved separately along the South wall:

1. Quick reference, including educational directories, career books, yearbooks, telephone directories, specialised encyclopaedias.
2. General encyclopaedias.
3. General mono- and bilingual dictionaries in English, German, French, Italian, Spanish and Russian, shelved by language only.
4. Specialist dictionaries, shelved in class number (i.e. subject) order.

Bibliographies are kept at the front of the issue desk and atlases on a stand nearby. A small collection of heavily used books is kept on 'short loan' at the issue desk. These may only be used in the Library and are available on request.

Periodicals and Newspapers

1. All items in Minor Languages are shelved at the end of their respective book sections.
2. Current issues of English newspapers, and of several periodicals in heavy demand, are kept at the library desk.
3. Other current issues are arranged on racks corresponding to the major area studies sections.
4. Back issues, except those in Minor Languages, are shelved alphabetically, periodicals in boxes and newspapers on wall racks.

Audio-visual collection

The Library has a collection of records, cassettes and tapes covering language and literature. They are listed in the card catalogue under 'Audio-visual'. Please ask at the issue desk if you wish to borrow one, or if you wish to use a listening room.

Registration

Please complete a yellow registration card and present your student identity card.

Borrowing

Up to 10 books may be borrowed for 3 weeks at a time. In addition back numbers of periodicals and 1 cassette **or** 1 or 2 records (depending on size) may be borrowed for 1 week. An issue slip must be completed for each non-book item. If not required by another reader, books may be renewed, but telephone renewals will not normally be accepted.

Reservations

If an item is not on the shelves a request card may be completed at the issue desk. The reader will be notified when it becomes available. Books and periodicals can also sometimes be obtained through the Inter-Library Loan service.

Photocopying

A self-service machine is available, subject to copyright regulations. It is operated by a meter, available from the issue desk. Copies cost 5p a sheet.

37 This passage gives information on library services for

    A   translators in a bureau.

    B   students at college.

    C   interpreters at a conference.

    D   teachers in a school.

38 If you wanted to consult a Chinese dictionary you would look for it

    A   at the end of the Chinese section.

    B   under a classified number.

    C   in alphabetical order.

    D   before the other books in Chinese.

39 Suppose you wished to look at the latest issue of a popular periodical. Where would you find it?

    A   In a wall rack.

    B   Stored in a box.

    C   At the library desk.

    D   Shelved alphabetically.

40 At the languages library it is possible to borrow

    A   ten books only, at any one time, for three weeks.

    B   books, a cassette and two records at the same time.

    C   several periodicals, a record and ten books all together.

    D   ten books, a number of periodicals and a cassette, for only one week.

PAPER 2   COMPOSITION (1½ hours)

Write **two only** *of the following composition exercises. Your answers must follow exactly the instructions given, and must be of between 120 and 180 words each.*

1   You have booked a place at an English Summer School. Unfortunately you cannot now attend. Write a letter of cancellation, giving your reasons for cancelling.

2   Give some advice to a friend who has consulted you about a new job.

3   Describe someone that you have met while learning English.

4   Which is the more powerful – the spoken or the written word?

5   (See Appendix : Prescribed texts)

PAPER 3   USE OF ENGLISH (2 hours)

SECTION A

1   *Fill each of the numbered blanks in the following passage. Use only **one** word in each space.*

Emma still faced the .... (1) they had come, with her back to the boys. She hooked the earpieces of the glasses .... (2) her ears so that the lenses were under her chin. She knew .... (3) she only wanted to put them on .... (4) she had been told not to, but at the .... (5) time she couldn't believe that looking .... (6) them for one short moment .... (7) damage her eyes.

She .... (8) she had a mirror with her. She thought she would like to put the glasses on and .... (9) take a quick look at herself, all wise and important .... (10) the owlish lenses. So she gave up the struggle and put the glasses .... (11) properly.

To her surprise .... (12) did not blur and ripple as she had expected it .... (13). She continued to look at the village and she saw it as clearly as .... (14). The only difference .... (15) that all round the .... (16) of her vision the golden frames .... (17) in the sun. She was .... (18) to ask the other two how she looked, but .... (19) she turned she saw that something was moving towards .... (20) along the track from the farm.

2   *Finish each of the following sentences in such a way that it means exactly the same as the sentence printed before it.*

> EXAMPLE: I've never been to America before.
>
> ANSWER: This is *the first time that I've ever been to America.*

a)   The police ordered the crowds to move on.

The crowds ....

b)   I've been learning English since I was twelve.

I first ....

c)   He was very upset when she ignored him.

She upset ....

d)   The buses couldn't move because of the traffic jams.

The traffic jams ....

e)   The weather was too cold for us to go out.

We ....

f)   She didn't write, so he forgot her.

If ....

g)   I'm sorry but I can't come tomorrow.

I apologise for ....

h)   Stephen is easily the best linguist in the class.

Nobody ....

i)   How did you manage to finish so fast?

What ....

j)   I haven't got enough money to buy that coat.

That coat ....

3 *Complete the following sentences with* **one** *appropriate word for a type of roadway.*

EXAMPLE: Our village is being destroyed by heavy traffic. There should be a
bypass round it.

a) The traffic only goes in one direction down a one-way ....

b) You should overtake in the fast .... on the motorway.

c) There was a long curving .... leading up to the house.

d) The dark, narrow .... in between the old houses led down to the harbour.

e) Generally, ... are lined on both sides by trees.

f) In the springtime it is lovely to walk down a country .... and see the blossom.

g) There was only a single sheep .... leading across the lonely moors.

h) Look, there's a sign. Let's take the .... across the fields.

4 *Write out the following passage in dialogue form, making all the necessary changes. Begin as shown.*

When Peter discovered that Suzanne was still working late at night he was very surprised and asked her what she was doing. She replied that she was studying hard for her English examination. Peter wanted to know why she was doing it so late, so she explained that she had not worked very hard until then and that she was trying to catch up. Peter commented that he could think of better things to do at night than study, to which Suzanne replied that that was typical of him. She then explained that if she could pass the examination then she stood a good chance of getting a better job. Peter was not very impressed by her reason and still insisted that there was more to life than just working. Suzanne said that as Peter's father was a company director, then presumably he, Peter, did not have to worry about getting a job. At which Peter expressed the opinion that the last thing he would ever do, would be to work for his father.

Peter: *Still working, Suzanne! What are you doing?*

Suzanne: *I'm studying hard for my examinations.*

Peter: ....

....

....

....

....

....

....

....

....

....

....

....

5 *Make all the changes and additions necessary to produce, from the following eight sets of words and phrases, eight sentences which together make a complete letter. Note carefully from the example what kind of alterations need to be made. Write each sentence in the space provided.*

EXAMPLE: I/be/Chief Accountant/Stubbs/ten years.

ANSWER: *I have been Chief Accountant at Stubbs for ten years.*

Dear Sir,

My firm/move/Colchester/autumn/next year.

a) ....

I/look/house/in the area/which/be/near schools, shops and public transport.

b) ....

My family/consists/myself/wife/four children so we/have/at least/five bedrooms and/large garden.

c) ....

I/be/glad/know/if/you/have/anything/suitable/offer/me.

d) ....

I/not afford/more than/£60,000 but I/not require/mortgage.

e) ....

I/be/Chief Accountant/Stubbs and they/be/glad/supply/reference.

f) ....

I/be/glad/if/you/get in touch/me/soon as possible.

g) ....

My office telephone number/be/01-207 7272 but I/prefer/you/telephone/me/home/evenings 01-584 7676.

h) ....

Yours faithfully,   *John Grant*

SECTION B

6 *Using only the information given in the holiday brochure, write three paragraphs continuing the conversation about holidays between Anne and Betty. Write about 50 words for each paragraph.*

RESIDENTIAL ADVENTURE HOLIDAYS

YOUNG ADVENTURER

AGES	8-12 YRS & 13-16 YRS
CENTRES	RIVER DART COUNTRY PARK, DEVON

One of the most exhilarating adventure holidays with Dolphin for 1984. The Holiday provides an unparalleled range of outdoor adventure activities which will thrill even the most demanding of youngsters.

In complete safety and under very experienced supervision, children can take part in rock climbing, abseiling, raft races, grass sledging and caving.

Friendly support coupled with experienced guidance ensures that everyone participates to the full in the adventure and fun.

A special feature of our evening programme at River Dart is an overnight Camp-out with camp fire cooking and songs!

LIST OF ACTIVITIES AVAILABLE

CAVING	GRASS SLEDGING
CANOEING	SWIMMING
CLIMBING	BOULDER HOPPING
ARCHERY	COMPUTING
RIFLE SHOOTING	BARBEQUES
HIGH ROPES COURSE	WIDE GAMES
HORSE RIDING	RAFT RACES
MOTOR SPORTS	VOLLEYBALL
ABSEILING	ASSAULT COURSE
ORIENTEERING	

TYPICAL DAYS PROGRAMME: YOUNG ADVENTURER

BREAKFAST ROCK CLIMBING AT LEIGHTOR, ABSEILING **LUNCH** GRASS SLEDGING, RAFT RACES, TRIAL BIKES **DINNER** OVERNIGHT CAMP

■ YOUNG ADVENTURER

CENTRE	DEVON
AGES	8-12, 13-16
PRICE	**£139**(+VAT)
STARTING DATES	JULY 21, 28 AUG 4, 11, 18, 25

SUPERSPORTS

AGES	8-12 YRS & 13-16 YRS
CENTRES	BRIGHTON, HARROGATE

Supersports is a sports intensive and coaching holiday for the fun loving, outgoing, and energetic. It allows you to concentrate on the best fun and most exciting sports and to get professional coaching throughout the week. We provide coaching in all the sports listed below and all our motor sports are included in the holiday cost.

Our young and friendly sports coaches are also group leaders who will help you through the week and encourage you in group competitions which culminate in the famous Dolphin all day "Superstars".

You will develop new sporting interests and skills throughout the week and will beat allcomers when you get back home.

LIST OF ACTIVITIES AVAILABLE

TRIAL BIKES	CANOEING
GO-KARTING	WINDSURFING
ARCHERY	SWIMMING
TENNIS	BMX BIKES
RIFLE SHOOTING	JUDO
SAILING	COMPUTING
BADMINTON	ROLLER SKATING
BASKETBALL	WATER POLO
VOLLEYBALL	

TYPICAL DAYS PROGRAMME: SUPERSPORTS

BREAKFAST TENNIS, TRIAL BIKES **LUNCH** SQUASH, ARCHERY, SWIMMING GALA **DINNER** COMPUTER/VIDEO GAMES

■ SUPERSPORTS

CENTRES	BRIGHTON	HARROGATE
AGES	8-12	13-16
PRICE	**£134** (+VAT)	
STARTING DATES	JULY 21, 28 AUG 4, 11, 18, 25	

RESIDENTIAL ADVENTURE HOLIDAYS

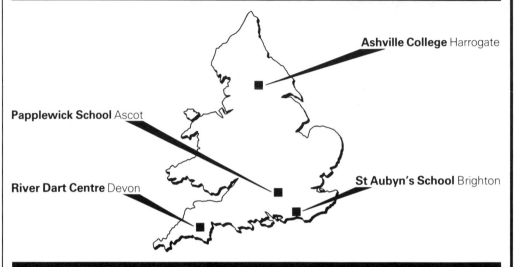

Ashville College Harrogate

Papplewick School Ascot

River Dart Centre Devon

St Aubyn's School Brighton

TEEN CAMP

AGES	13-16 YRS
CENTRES	BRIGHTON, HARROGATE AND ASCOT

A new Dolphin Holiday specially developed for todays teenagers. Not only have the activities been chosen to appeal to you, but the whole style of the Holiday is designed to be informal and relaxed. It is up to you to decide what you want to try and then to concentrate on the things you like most. Badminton, sailing, archery, computing and squash are just a sample of what you can do within this highly stimulating adventure holiday.

What is assured is that you will have a great time, both with young people of your own age and with our staff who are chosen not just for their ability to pass on skills to you, but because we know that you'll all get on well together.

There will be evening programmes for you as well, like specially chosen films, barbeques and discos.

LIST OF ACTIVITIES AVAILABLE

TENNIS	GYMNASTICS
BADMINTON	COMPUTING
TABLE TENNIS	FOOTBALL
TEAM SPORTS	BMX BIKES
SWIMMING	ROLLER SKATING
SAILING	RIDING (£5 per session)
ARCHERY	ORIENTEERING
CANOEING	PHOTOGRAPHY
JUDO	RIFLE SHOOTING
TRAMPOLINING	T-SHIRT DESIGN
AEROBICS	VOLLEYBALL
SQUASH	WATER POLO
BASKETBALL	VIDEO

TYPICAL DAYS PROGRAMME: TEEN CAMP
BREAKFAST ROLLER SKATING, TENNIS **LUNCH** COMPUTING, SWIMMING, RIFLE-SHOOTING **DINNER** DISCO

■ **TEEN CAMP**

CENTRES	BRIGHTON, HARROGATE, ASCOT
AGES	13-16
PRICE	**£126** (+VAT)
STARTING DATES	JULY 21, 28 AUG 4, 11, 18, 25

Anne: Where are you going for your holidays this year, Betty?

Betty: Well, we're going to Florence, but the children aren't keen, they don't like historic cities. We thought we might send them on one of the Dolphin holidays.

Anne: That's interesting, Jonathan wants to go to one of their camps too. He's into Martial Arts at the moment – you know, judo and karate. And, of course, he's absolutely mad about computers. But then I suppose all boys of twelve are nowadays.

Betty: Well, I think Peter must be the exception, he's all for physical excitement – scrabbling up mountains and anything to do with boats would be his idea of fun – and he's only eleven! Whereas Carol's just the opposite. She doesn't like being near the sea or rivers but adores dancing and horses. Still, at fourteen she won't want to go to the same place as Peter.

Anne: So where are you sending her?

Betty: ....

....

....

....

....

Anne: And Peter?

Betty: ....

....

....

....

....

What about Jonathan, where's he going?

Anne: ....

....

....

....

....

PAPER 4   LISTENING COMPREHENSION (20 to 30 minutes)

FIRST PART

Fill in the information you hear on the form below. Some of it has been filled in for you.

Exhibition Organisation

How Satisfied?	Very Satisfied	Satisfied	Moderately Satisfied	Not Satisfied because:
Layout of exhibition	4	3	2	✓ computers too far from video
① Catering arrangements	4	3	2	1 ....
② Parking facilities	4	3	2	1 ....
Heating/ lighting	4	3	2	✗ too hot / too bright
③ Opening times	4	3	2	1 ....

④ How did you travel to the exhibition? ....

⑤ How long did you stay at the exhibition? ....

General Comments

⑥ Please specify high and low points of overall satisfaction and indicate any serious omissions.

Do you consider that the exhibition could be improved?

(i) Yes ✓

(ii) No

⑦ If (i) how? ......*stands not as close* / .... / ....

SECOND PART

For questions 8–19 tick (√) whether the statements are true or false.

	True	False

8   Young people go to nomadic clubs just to drink.

9   The Circus has been going for less than three years.

10   Jeremy, the DJ, plays highly original discs.

11   The clubs are held in unusual places.

12   The Circus advertises to keep itself exclusive.

13   The Dirtbox has only a small following.

14   Phil and Bob do not bother to decorate their club.

15   The music at The Dirtbox is unpredictable.

16   The Substation thinks that luxury is unimportant.

17   You can watch silent films at The Substation.

18   You can stay at the club until breakfast time.

19   It is difficult for the police to find the clubs.

THIRD PART

First look at this Student Services notice from an educational college, then fill in the missing information by writing short answers to the questions 20–29 that follow.

STUDENT SERVICES

Information leaflet No.2

PART-TIME WORK

WESTMINSTER COLLEGE

Opening times – Open most days

Drop in without an appointment

For messages – leave in

the book in the office

---

20 From a non-EEC country—want part-time work in Britain. What should I do?

....

21 Passport says I cannot work, and I do so. What could happen? ....

....

22 Where should I go to look for part-time work? ....

23 Where are jobs advertised daily? ....

24 Why visit the Catering Job Centre? ....

25 What must I do well to work in an office? ....

26 Who should I contact if I want to work in a cinema? ....

27 What is the age limit for an au pair? ....

28 Approximately how much of my earnings will be taken off in tax? ....

....

29 What happens if I work less than a full tax year? ....

PAPER 5   INTERVIEW (12 to 15 minutes)

SECTION A: PICTURE CONVERSATION

Look at this picture carefully and be prepared to answer some questions about it.

(See Teacher's Edition for suggested questions and topics.)

SECTION B: READING PASSAGE

Look at this passage and be prepared to answer some questions about it and then to read it aloud.

Ladies and gentlemen, I feel deeply honoured to receive this award tonight. But without the help and support of my editor and publisher this book would never have been written. I am very excited to have the chance of using the money for travelling. It will help me realise a long-cherished ambition to visit China – the scene of my next book. Thank you.

(See Teacher's Edition for suggested questions.)

SECTION C: STRUCTURED COMMUNICATION ACTIVITY

There may be a variety of options offered in this section. Choose one of the following:

a) Imagine that you are at a railway station waiting for a train to Dover. You hear an announcement but are not quite sure what it said, although it mentioned something about delays on the Dover line. Ask someone to help you.

    Find out: about the delay on the Dover line.
                  why your train is delayed.
                  if there is another way to get to Dover.
                  how long you are likely to have to wait.
                  if there is anywhere to have a drink or a meal while you wait.
                  whether you can use your ticket on another route.

b) Group or pair work.

    The examiner is going to think of a wild animal. You must ask questions to find out which animal it is. You are allowed up to twenty questions. The examiner can only answer 'yes' or 'no' to your questions.

c) (See Appendix : Prescribed texts)

Test Four

PAPER 1   READING COMPREHENSION (1 hour)

This paper is in two parts, section A and section B. For each question you answer correctly in section A you gain **one** *mark; for each question you answer correctly in section B you gain* **two** *marks. No marks are deducted for wrong answers. Answer all the questions. Indicate your choice of answer in every case on the separate answer sheet, which should show your name and examination index number. Follow carefully the instructions about how to record your answers.*

SECTION A

In this section you must choose the word or phrase which best completes each sentence. For each question, 1 to 25, indicate on your answer sheet the letter A, B, C or D against the number of the question.

1   The boy was .... by the noise of the explosion.
    A afraid   B nervous   C frightened   D fearful

2   She realised she had .... her handbag in the library.
    A forgotten   B left   C mistaken   D remembered

3   If there's one thing I don't like, it's .... tea.
    A pale   B delicate   C light   D weak

4   There will be .... showers in the South-East during the day.
    A sprinkled   B scattered   C interrupted   D dispersed

5   We shall have to .... if we want to go to Florida this summer.
    A save up   B put away   C put aside   D lay up

6   What was the film .... ?
    A concerning   B of   C about   D describing

7   How do you like your eggs .... ?
    A done   B made   C set   D ready

8   It was .... work building the bridge in that hot climate.
    A powerful   B strong   C hard   D vigorous

9   Sooner or later he will have to .... his responsibilities.
    A face up to   B take account   C look after   D see into

10 I can't .... why he turned that job down.
    A suppose   B fancy   C realise   D imagine

11 If you've got a headache, why don't you take a .... of aspirin?
    A pair   B couple   C brace   D couplet

12 The accommodation was cheap, but the food was very ....
    A costly   B high   C dear   D overpaid

13 To be honest, I've never .... been to a horror film.
    A truly   B actually   C genuinely   D currently

14 Children and pensioners are admitted to the museum at .... prices.
    A undercharged   B less   C reduced   D decreased

15 My alarm clock goes .... at seven o'clock every morning.
    A on   B out   C in   D off

16 The price quoted .... room with bath and breakfast.
    A costs   B consists   C includes   D contains

17 Owing to the exceptionally cold weather, there has been a very .... harvest
    this year.
    A poor   B little   C mean   D seedy

18 I hope the weather will .... before we leave for Brighton.
    A clear off   B go off   C clear up   D go away

19 The teacher sent him out of the room because he .... in class.
    A misconducted   B misbehaved   C misled   D misinformed

20 Do put on your coat, or you may catch .... in this wind.
    A fever   B cough   C illness   D cold

21 The Minister stated that he could not .... with the arguments for nuclear
    defence.
    A admit   B accept   C agree   D assent

22 All cigarette packets carry .... about the effects of smoking on health.
    A an advice   B an alarm   C a warning   D an alert

23 According to the weather .... , it's going to be fine today.
    A prediction   B indication   C announcement   D forecast

24 I noticed .... smell when I opened the refrigerator.
    A an amusing   B a comical   C an absurd   D a funny

25 Please keep all medicines out of .... of children.
    A reach   B arm's length   C range   D grasp

SECTION B

In this section you will find after each of the passages a number of questions or unfinished statements about the passage, each with four suggested answers or ways of finishing. You must choose the one which you think fits best. For each question, 26 to 40, indicate on your answer sheet the letter A, B, C or D against the number of the question.

FIRST PASSAGE

Shrove Tuesday is the day before the beginning of Lent, the 40-day period before Easter in the Christian year. It is celebrated in many different ways all over the world, but in England is traditionally associated with the cooking and eating of pancakes – so much so that it is often called Pancake Day.

At Olney, a small town in England, Shrove Tuesday is Pancake Race Day. The race is said to have first been run there in 1445 and has continued more or less ever since with occasional interruptions as, for example, during the Second World War.

It is a race for women only. They must be housewives and live in the area. They have to cook a pancake and run about 400 metres from the village square to the parish church, tossing their pancake three times as they run. They have to wear aprons and cover their heads with a hat or scarf. A bell rings twice for the women to start making their pancakes and then again for them to assemble in the square, carrying their cooked pancakes in a frying pan. There they wait for the bell to ring again and the race starts. Sometimes one of the pancakes drops on the ground, but the runner is allowed to pick it up and toss it again. The winner and the runner-up both get a prize from the vicar who is waiting at the church door. The verger, who helps to look after the church, gets a kiss from the winner—and often her pancake as well. Then all the runners take their frying pans with the pancakes into the church and a short service is held.

The pancake race, with the women flying along, tossing and trying to catch their pancakes, provides a great deal of entertainment and is frequently shown on television. In 1950, a similar pancake race was organised in Kansas, USA, and has continued ever since. It takes place on the same day, at exactly the same time. Times are clocked on both sides of the Atlantic and there is keen competition to see whether the British or American housewives run fastest.

26 It is believed that the pancake race

    A   has been held every year since 1445.

    B   dates back to the 15th century.

    C   originated in the 14th century.

    D   started after the Second World War.

27 The race is only open to women who

    A   are staying in the area.

    B   got married in Olney.

    C   maintain a home in the district.

    D   were born in Olney.

28 During the race, the competitors have to

    A   jump three times and catch a pancake.

    B   toss the pancakes to each other.

    C   throw some pancakes into a frying pan.

    D   throw and catch their pancakes.

29 According to the rules, the women must

    A   hide their faces under a hat.

    B   cover part of their clothes.

    C   put an apron round their head.

    D   cover their faces with a scarf.

30 When the race is over, all the runners

    A   are presented with prayer books.

    B   serve pancakes in the church.

    C   conduct a service.

    D   take part in a ceremony.

31 Since 1950, women in Kansas, USA, have

    A   taken part in the Olney race.

    B   clocked up a Pancake Day record.

    C   competed against the Olney women.

    D   organised other Pancake Day festivities.

SECOND PASSAGE

Dear Sir,

As one of your regular readers, I have always admired your policy of supporting the problems of the ordinary citizens of London. I hope, therefore, that you will find space to publish this letter. I live in a tower block in the East End of London, situated between two busy streets with a street market along its third side. Naturally we suffer from traffic, noise, dirt and petrol fumes. However, behind us we have an open green space with shady trees which provides us with a quiet, pleasant place where we can enjoy our leisure hours. We are mostly pensioners and there are very few children on the estate.

Our local council recently proposed to make use of this site as a temporary play centre for about 100 children. Although all the residents strongly protested against this plan, the council have totally ignored us and have already started uprooting our trees and grass, in spite of the fact that there is a disused school and playground within 100 metres which would suit their purpose equally well. I should be glad to hear from other readers who have had similar problems and might be able to advise us on what action we should now take.

P. Greene,
12 Gilmore Street, E1

32 This letter is addressed to a

    A   newspaper correspondent.

    B   housing manager.

    C   daily newspaper.

    D   local councillor.

33 The writer lives in

    A   a block of houses.

    B   a busy traffic zone.

    C   a secluded area.

    D   the Tower of London.

34 The residents on the estate

    A are mostly retired. ✓

    B are partially disabled.

    C have no children.

    D live by themselves.

35 The council proposed to

    A build a school on the site.

    B use the site for a sports ground.

    C make short-term use of the site.

    D only admit children to the site.

36 Since the residents' protest, the council have

    A had second thoughts.

    B demolished the area.

    C gone ahead with their plans.

    D revised their original plan.

THIRD PASSAGE

37 This exhibition is most likely to interest

    A   research scientists.

    B   company managers.

    C   technical writers.

    D   telephone operators.

38 The exhibitors believe that there is a need for more

    A   technological development.

    B   computer trainees.

    C   business commitments.

    D   knowledge of technology.

39 Visitors to the exhibition will be expected to

    A   examine a number of possibilities.

    B   place orders for office machines.

    C   make certain undertakings.

    D   be familiar with new technology.

40 The exhibition is open

    A   every four years.

    B   four times a year.

    C   for four days a year.

    D   for four years.

PAPER 2   COMPOSITION (1½ hours)

*Write **two only** of the following composition exercises. Your answers must follow exactly the instructions given, and must be of between 120 and 180 words each.*

1   You have received a letter from a friend asking you to lend him/her £100 towards the deposit on a new car. Reply to this letter explaining why in your present circumstances you are unable to do this.

2   Explain to a friend the advantages and disadvantages of living alone.

3   What do you consider to be the best way to keep fit?

4   Describe what, in your opinion, are the qualities and abilities that make a good teacher.

5   (See Appendix: Prescribed texts)

PAPER 3   USE OF ENGLISH (2 hours)

SECTION A

1   *Fill each of the numbered blanks in the following passage. Use only* **one** *word in each space.*

Research has .... (1) that excessive noise damages .... (2) hearing. In fact many young people now .... (3) from deafness from regularly going to discos .... (4) the level of noise is .... (5) high that they have to shout to make themselves .... (6). Unfortunately, in spite .... (7) modern technology, noise is very .... (8) part of our modern world – planes .... (9) overhead, traffic thundering .... (10) busy roads, television, portable radios, all produce noise .... (11) which we have become so accustomed that we hardly notice .... (12). In fact people going on country holidays have .... (13) known to complain that it is .... (14) quiet. They actually .... (15) the noises they are used to in their daily lives. The problem is that noise, ... (16) it does not necessarily cause deafness, causes stress and this .... (17) in the long run prove harmful. However, the decision about more or .... (18) noise cannot be .... (19) to the scientists alone. It is .... (20) to us to decide what kind of world we want to live in.

2 *Finish each of the following sentences in such a way that it means exactly the same as the sentence printed before it.*

EXAMPLE: 'Where do you live?' I asked John.

ANSWER: I asked *John where he lived.*

a) He performed very well in *Macbeth*.

His performance ....

b) It rained all the time when we were on holiday.

It never ....

c) We shall soon be in London.

It won't ....

d) He didn't do as badly in the test as he expected.

He did ....

e) No one ever saw him again.

He ....

f) They almost missed the plane.

They very ....

g) Did you pay a lot for that coat?

Was that coat ....

h) He didn't seem to understand me.

I don't ....

i) John promised to phone Mary that evening.

'I'll ....

j) That farm once belonged to my grandfather.

My grandfather ....

3   *Complete the following sentences with the correct preposition or particle.*

EXAMPLE: He ran *away* to sea when he was fourteen.

a)   Don't you think Susie takes .... her mother?

b)   The thieves made .... with £150,000 in cash.

c)   Hold .... a minute. I'll put you through.

d)   The regulations are very clearly set .... in the leaflet.

e)   They are giving .... a bottle of perfume with every order over five pounds.

4   *Write out the following passage in dialogue form, making all necessary changes. Begin as shown.*

Mrs Birch wanted to know why her young son, Johnny, was so late. It was half-past six and he had never been so late home from school before. Johnny apologised and explained that all the buses were full up, so he had had to walk most of the way home. Mrs Birch said that she didn't believe it could have taken him so long and, anyway, he knew she didn't like him walking home alone in the dark. Johnny explained that he hadn't been alone. Two of his friends had been with him and they had stopped to have a coffee at Ken's café. Mrs Birch suggested he hadn't only stopped for a coffee, but had been playing on the computer games in the café. Johnny admitted that they had had a go on one of them. He went on to say that it was a new one where you had to try and capture a gigantic spider from outer space. Mrs Birch told him he was talking rubbish but Johnny insisted that it was true and described the spider as having electronic legs and laser-beam eyes. When Johnny asked if he could watch the sports programme on TV while he was having his supper, Mrs Birch refused sharply and ordered him to eat his supper and then do his homework.

Mrs Birch: *Why are you so late, Johnny? It's half-past six. You've never been home from school so late before.*

Johnny: *I'm sorry. All the buses were full up, so I had to walk most of the way home.*

Mrs Birch: ....

....

....

....

....

....

....

....

....

....

....

....

....

....

....

....

5   *Make all the changes and additions necessary to produce, from the following eight sets of words and phrases, eight sentences which together make the introduction to the radio programme 'City Life Question Time'. Note carefully from the example what kind of alterations need to be made. Write each sentence in the space provided.*

EXAMPLE: We be/pleased/welcome/Joanna Lawson/our programme.

ANSWER: *We are pleased to welcome Joanna Lawson to our programme.*

Since/Joanna Lawson/last/take/part/this programme/she/spend/study/ housing problems.

a)   ....

I be/sure/she/be/able/answer/many/the/questions/our audience/want/ask.

b)   ....

She/know/personal experience/how/difficult/it/be/find/cheap accommodation/ big city.

c)   ....

This week/we/go/deal/particularly/problems/young single people.

d)   ....

It/seem/their special needs/never/fully/understand/people/plan/our cities.

e)   ....

Many/young people/oblige/live/rooms/lack/cooking/toilet/facilities.

f)   ....

They/often/find/themselves/pay/excessive rents/greedy landlords.

g)   ....

Now/we/like/have/first question/Mr Robert Peters/come/East London.

h)   ....

SECTION B

6 *Using the information given in the following advertisements, continue each of the four paragraphs in the spaces provided. Use about 50 words for each paragraph.*

ISLINGTON HEALTH AUTHORITY
WHITTINGTON HOSPITAL

SECRETARY
(HIGHER CLERICAL OFFICER)

To provide a secretarial support to the Unit Administrator. The unit comprises the Royal Northern and Whittington Hospitals and so this post involves contact with a wide range of staff as well as with the public. As well as involving the usual secretarial/administrative work this post gives the opportunity to use your initiative, and common sense is vital. Good secretarial skills are required, including shorthand, and knowledge of a word processor would be useful.
Salary scale: £5,723–£6,712 inclusive.

THEATRE STERILE SUPPLIES UNIT ASSISTANT
GRADE 2

Interesting work involving assembly of surgical instruments and supplying operating theatres. Previous experience not necessary but common sense and willingness to do some shift work and alternate Saturday mornings is essential. Basic weekly wage £82.18 (extra payments made for weekend and overtime working).
For an informal visit contact Mr Giblin, TSSU Manager, on 01-272 3070, ext 4454. Job description and application form available from Hospital Personnel Department, Whittington Hospital, St Mary's Wing, Highgate Hill, London, N19. Tel. 01-272 9679

05

As well as providing secretarial support to ....

....

....

....

....

The successful applicant for the first post will need ....

....

....

....

....

The assistant in the Theatre Sterile Supplies Unit will ....

....

....

....

....

To find out more about both jobs ....

....

....

....

PAPER 4   LISTENING COMPREHENSION (20 to 30 minutes)

FIRST PART

For each of questions 1–5 put a tick (√) in one of the boxes, A, B, C or D.

1   The house plants should be kept

   A   in a sunny position.

   B   away from draughts.

   C   in the shade.

   D   in a hot place.

A
B
C
D

2   To encourage growth, the earth needs to be kept

   A   very wet.

   B   fairly damp.

   C   rather cool.

   D   quite dry.

A
B
C
D

3   The salesman advises feeding the plant

   A   every week.

   B   in April and September only.

   C   every six months.

   D   during the summer months.

A
B
C
D

4   The pot plant may make marks if it is put on

   A   wooden furniture.

   B   polished containers.

   C   greasy tables.

   D   a hard surface.

A
B
C
D

5   How much did Mary pay for the house plant?

   A   £4.65

   B   £3.50

   C   £15.00

   D   £5.00

A
B
C
D

SECOND PART

For questions 6–10 put a tick (√) in one of the boxes A, B, C or D.

6   This announcement is being made at a

    A   public auction.

    B   Christmas party.

    C   charity fair.

    D   children's party.

A
B
C
D

7   The money raised is for the benefit of

    A   injured people.

    B   hospital patients.

    C   children in care.

    D   disabled children.

A
B
C
D

8   The speaker introduces

    A   a local personality.

    B   a TV star.

    C   the Mayor of Ditton.

    D   a social worker.

A
B
C
D

9   The public have bought tickets for a

    A   prize giving.

    B   presentation.

    C   lottery.

    D   reward.

A
B
C
D

10   Tony Myers is going to

    A   select the prizes.

    B   draw the winners.

    C   pull out the prizes.

    D   choose the winners.

A
B
C
D

THIRD PART

*For question 11 number the instructions for making bread in the correct order
1−8. Put the number in the box. The first one has been done for you.*

11	a Knead mixture and leave to rise.	
	b Put in the oven to bake.	
	c Add sugar and yeast to lukewarm water.	1
	d Knead again and shape into loaves.	
	e Add the yeast mixture to the flour and salt.	
	f Take out of oven after 45 minutes.	
	g Leave mixture till bubbly. Add fat.	
	h Put in baking tins. Leave to double in size.	

For questions 12−15 write in the missing word for each of the sentences.

12 Clare is .... the dough.

13 She shapes the mixture into ....

14 Wait till the dough has ....

15 The dough rises to .... its size.

16 The .... and salt were already in the bowl.

PAPER 5 INTERVIEW (12 to 15 minutes)

SECTION A: PICTURE CONVERSATION

Look at this picture carefully and be prepared to answer some questions about it.

(See Teacher's Edition for suggested questions and topics.)

SECTION B: READING PASSAGE

Look at this passage and be prepared to answer some questions about it and then to read it aloud.

You will have been asked at check-in whether or not you want to smoke. Should you find that you are sitting in the wrong part of the aircraft, please wait until you have been airborne for about ten minutes, then ask the crew if you can move. Remember, at no time is smoking permitted in the toilet areas or when you are standing in the aisles.

(See Teacher's Edition for suggested questions.)

SECTION C: STRUCTURED COMMUNICATION ACTIVITY

There may be a variety of options offered in this section. Choose one of the following:

a) You are at the dry-cleaner's. You want to have a new zip put into your favourite casual jacket and a grease stain removed. The examiner is the assistant at the dry-cleaner's.

   Say: what you want done.

   Explain: what the stain is.

   Ask: how much it will cost.
         when it will be ready.

b) Group or pair work.
   Discuss how to look after yourself and make friends if you are living alone in a strange city.

   Suggestions: meals
               budgeting for bills
               sport
               evening classes
               youth clubs

c) (See Appendix : Prescribed texts)

Test Five

PAPER 1   READING COMPREHENSION (1 hour)

*This paper is in two parts, section A and section B. For each question you answer correctly in section A you gain **one** mark; for each question you answer correctly in section B you gain **two** marks. No marks are deducted for wrong answers. Answer all the questions. Indicate your choice of answer in every case on the separate answer sheet, which should show your name and examination index number. Follow carefully the instructions about how to record your answers.*

SECTION A

In this section you must choose the word or phrase which best completes each sentence. For each question, 1 to 25, indicate on your answer sheet the letter A, B, C or D against the number of the question.

1   You can .... on John to look after things while you are away.
    A believe   B count   C presume   D trust

2   He had three .... when he went to the dentist.
    A fillings   B stoppages   C stuffings   D blockages

3   The river .... east to the sea.
    A rolls   B moves   C pours   D flows

4   She never learnt the piano but she can play by ....
    A heart   B hand   C ear   D memory

5   They always .... extra staff in the summer season.
    A put on   B take in   C put in   D take on

6   They made .... of £1,000 on the sale of their house.
    A a gain   B a profit   C a benefit   D an increase

7   She's always .... up trouble between friends.
    A stirring   B mixing   C making   D doing

8   Mrs Parker was .... tired that she fell asleep in the train.
    A too   B such   C so   D very

9   .... children are not admitted to this film.
    A Unattached   B Unaccompanied   C Unattended   D Unrelated

10 I don't know .... he works.
    A which   B what   C who   D where

11 That book has been out of .... for a long time.
    A press   B print   C publication   D copy

12 He was .... asleep when the alarm went off.
    A sound   B completely   C profoundly   D deep

13 It was .... a beautiful evening, I decided to walk home.
    A so   B even   C such   D just

14 Our tourist guide knew London like the back of her ....
    A head   B hand   C heart   D heel

15 Her blue dress .... the colour of her eyes.
    A equalled   B paired   C fitted   D matched

16 Traffic on the motorway has been reduced to two ....
    A lanes   B roads   C ways   D paths

17 Liverpool are sure to .... Manchester United in the match on Saturday.
    A win   B overcome   C beat   D gain

18 I can't remember his name but it's on the ....
    A top of my head   B front of my eyes   C tip of my tongue
    D end of my nose

19 Mary asked the shopkeeper to put the vegetables in a ....
    A holdall   B handbag   C satchel   D carrier bag

20 When I first started work, I found her advice ....
    A priceless   B invaluable   C worthy   D irreplaceable

21 Our flight was .... from Heathrow to Manchester Airport.
    A replaced   B reverted   C deflected   D diverted

22 The criminal has a .... on his right cheek.
    A scar   B sign   C trace   D point

23 You can get there .... crossing that bridge.
    A by   B from   C with   D on

24 They have .... music at that disco.
    A real   B live   C actual   D living

25 You'd better take an extra £10 .... you need it for taxis.
    A unless   B in spite of   C in case   D though

SECTION B

In this section you will find after each of the passages a number of questions or unfinished statements about the passage, each with four suggested answers or ways of finishing. You must choose the one which you think fits best. For each question, 26 to 40, indicate on your answer sheet the letter A, B, C or D against the number of the question.

FIRST PASSAGE

Prehistoric men and women enjoyed a more varied diet than people do now, since they ate species of plant and several hundred thousand types of living creature. But only a tiny percentage of these were ever domesticated. Modern shops have accelerated a trend towards specialisation which began in the earliest days of agriculture. The food of the rich countries has become cheaper relative to wages. It is speedily distributed in supermarkets. But the choice annually becomes less and less great. Even individual foods themselves become more standardised. We live in the world of the carrot specially blunted in order to avoid making a hole in the bag, and the tomato grown to meet a demand for a standard weight of eighteen tomatoes to a kilo. Siri von Reis Altschul asks: 'Only the three major cereals and perhaps ten other widely cultivated species stand between famine and survival for the world's human population and a handful of drug plants has served Western civilisation for several thousand years. A rather obvious question arises: are we missing something?' After all, there are 800,000 species of plant on earth.

26 In prehistoric times people
    A   ate much more than we do today.
    B   lived mainly on plant food.
    C   had a wide-ranging diet.
    D   had a wider choice of natural food.

27 Most of the food we eat today is
    A   meant to be eaten quickly.
    B   marketed without delay.
    C   eaten in the supermarket.
    D   intended for immediate consumption.

28 Most of us have become conditioned to expect
   A   no variation in our diet.
   B   a reduction in food supplies.
   C   a specialist diet.
   D   food conforming to a set standard.

29 According to the text, world population today survives on
   A   the products of Western civilisation.
   B   several thousand plants and cereals.
   C   a minimal number of cultivated foods.
   D   species planted one thousand years ago.

30 The conclusion seems to be that we
   A   could make use of more natural species.
   B   don't cultivate the right kind of food.
   C   produce more food than we need.
   D   cultivate too many different species.

Space test shatters scientists

from Erskine McCullough in Los Angeles

EXPERIMENTS aboard the space shuttle Columbia have shattered a theory on the human nervous system which won an Austrian professor a Nobel prize 69 years ago.

West German astronaut Ulf Merbold disproved the theory during tests aboard the space craft yesterday. His discovery relates to the workings of the inner ear, the body's balance mechanism.

In 1914 Professor Robert Barany won the Nobel prize for physiology and medicine when he announced that temperature differences affected the inner ear and caused the eyes to flicker. His theory was accepted by scientists.

But Merbold carried out tests to find if the theory was correct and stunned himself and space officials when he proved it wrong.

According to Barany's theory the eyes would flick when cold air was blown into one ear and hot air blown into the other.

But if this theory was correct such a movement would be impossible in zero gravity.

Both Merbold's eyes continually blinked when the test was carried out.

31 An accredited scientific theory has been

   A disproved by a Nobel prize-winner.

   B discovered in outer space.

   C tested in orbit.

   D approved by astronauts.

32 Professor Barany's theory claimed to prove

   A how our hearing mechanism works.

   B that eye movement is affected by temperature.

   C why we constantly move our eyes.

   D how hearing reacts to space conditions.

33 The inaccuracy of Barany's theory was proved in space by the effects of

   A weightlessness.

   B the pull of gravity.

   C loss of weight.

   D hot and cold air streams.

34 The result of the West German astronaut's tests was

   A regarded as improbable.

   B totally unexpected.

   C much as anticipated.

   D somewhat frightening.

CHILDREN ON BIKES

Cycling accidents often happen because children are allowed out on the roads before they're really ready. After all, it takes time to learn to ride a bike safely, and riding safely means much more than just staying on. For example, a child must be able to turn and look behind, and do hand signals without wobbling. And at the same time as handling the bike safely, the child must be able to cope with the roads and traffic.

How to prevent accidents

Make sure that your child's bike has the right size of frame and that the saddle and handlebars are correctly adjusted. When sitting on the saddle, a child's feet should comfortably touch the ground and hands must be able to work the brake levers.

Make sure children can ride safely and can cope with roads and traffic before you let them out alone. As a general rule, children under nine years old should never be allowed out on the roads on a bike alone. An adult should always be with them.

Encourage your child to go in for a Cycling Proficiency Test. You can get details of courses from your Road Safety Officer at your local authority. Look in your telephone directory for the local authority number. But remember that these courses are often run in school

playgrounds, so it's important to make sure that what's learnt is then put into practice on the roads.

Make sure that your child understands road signs. Explain, for example, that 'crossroads' does not mean 'cross the road'. Words like 'one-way street' and 'traffic island' can also be difficult for children to understand.

Teach your child about the dangers of:

1. Turning right
2. Riding off the pavement onto the road without looking
3. Roundabouts
4. Passing parked cars

5. Motorists coming out of side roads

Teach children to ride in single file on narrow roads or in traffic. Show them how to plan routes to avoid busy roads or tricky junctions.

Teach your child that it's dangerous to show off on a bike by riding with 'no hands'.

Cycling on the pavement is strictly speaking illegal. But it's accepted that it's safer for young children on tricycles or small bikes. Teach them to be careful of people walking on the pavement.

Make sure that your child wears reflective clothing when out on a bike, especially in the dark or in bad weather. For night-time riding, lights must be working and reflectors must be clean.

Bicycle maintenance can be life-saving. It's up to parents to check their children's bikes regularly and get repairs done properly. Teach your child, too, to check brakes and lights regularly.

A message to drivers

Children on bikes are often seriously injured by cars, buses and lorries. As a driver, be prepared for children to wobble or suddenly wander across your path. Always give them plenty of room. And, after parking, always look before you open your door.

35 Young children riding bicycles often find it difficult to

    A   recognise the correct signals.

    B   keep their balance when signalling.

    C   distinguish between right and left.

    D   keep their bike on the road.

36 When choosing a bike for a child, you should ensure that it

    A   has been specially made.

    B   has adjustable brakes.

    C   has a comfortable frame.

    D   is the right size.

37 The Cycling Proficiency Test

    A   is always held at the children's school.

    B   may only offer limited practice.

    C   is compulsory for all young cyclists.

    D   is organised by the school authorities.

38 Parents should teach their children about the dangers of

    A   riding in single file.

    B   riding without holding on.

    C   wearing luminous clothes.

    D   planning routes carefully.

39 It is the parent's responsibility to

    A   make sure the child repairs the bike.

    B   do all the repairs themselves.

    C   check that the bike is fit to use.

    D   clean the bike regularly.

40 Drivers must always

    A   be prepared to pass young cyclists.

    B   make room for cyclists to park.

    C   be on the look-out for young cyclists.

    D   try to prevent cyclists from passing.

PAPER 2   COMPOSITION (1½ hours)

*Write **two only** of the following composition exercises. Your answers must follow exactly the instructions given, and must be of between 120 and 180 words each.*

1   A friend has told you that there will shortly be a vacancy for a receptionist at the hotel where she works. Write a letter to the hotel manager enquiring about the job. Give your qualifications and experience and say why you think you would be suitable.

2   Another student is coming to share your flat. Write what you would say about the contributions you expect him/her to make towards food and expenses. Explain how the cooking and housework will be shared.

3   Computer games – education or entertainment?

4   What makes you laugh?

5   (See Appendix: Prescribed texts)

PAPER 3   USE OF ENGLISH (2 hours)

SECTION A

1   *Fill each of the numbered blanks in the following passage. Use only* **one** *word in each space.*

With a screeching of brakes, the car stopped outside the supermarket .... (1) the bank. Three masked men leapt out and raced across the road to the bank which was .... (2) opening. It was the early morning rush .... (3). Everyone was hurrying to work, so nobody in the street took .... (4) notice. The men pushed their way into the bank, slamming the door .... (5) them. Seconds .... (6) the alarm went .... (7). The men reappeared, dashed to their waiting car, ... (8) the driver already had the engine .... (9). They jumped in and the car took off, disappearing .... (10) the corner at top .... (11).

When the police arrived, they found two bank clerks shot in .... (12) chest, the manager locked in his office, hammering .... (13) the door and a third clerk .... (14) unconscious on the floor. It was he .... (15) had managed to sound the alarm .... (16) he was hit on the head with a gun.

The car was found .... (17) in a side street but the robbers are .... (18) at large. They got .... (19) with £140,000 in cash. The police have issued a description, but so .... (20) no one has come forward to help them with their enquiries.

Test Five

2   *Finish each of the following sentences in such a way that it means exactly the same as the sentence printed before it.*

EXAMPLE: Rembrandt painted this picture.

ANSWER: This picture *was painted by Rembrandt.*

a)   He plays football better than anyone in our team.

He is ....

b)   They had never met before.

It was ....

c)   'I've been waiting for you for half an hour, John,' said Mary irritably.

Mary complained ....

d)   There was a letter for you this morning.

A letter ....

e)   I like classical music better than pop.

I don't ....

f)   What's your height?

How ....

g)   Mary and I take a different size in shoes.

I don't ....

h)   No one ever discovered the identity of the murdered man.

The identity ....

i)   Joining a club is a good way to make friends.

A good way ....

j)   I advised Mark to go to the doctor's.

'You'd ....

3 *Complete each of the following sentences with the correct phrase made from* TURN.

> EXAMPLE: She *turned off* .... the television at midnight.

a) The party .... to be quite fun after all.

b) The road was blocked so we had to ....

c) The restaurant was so full that they were .... customers

....

d) He applied for the job but he was ....

4 *Complete each of the following sentences with the appropriate word beginning with* MIS.

> EXAMPLE: I'm afraid you *misunderstood* .... what I said.

a) I seem to have .... my keys.

b) The little boy .... in class so he was sent out.

c) It was a case of .... identity.

d) Your name has been .... on that document.

5 *Matthew is too fat. He is talking to his friend Douglas. Complete the dialogue.*

Douglas: If you want to lose some weight, why don't you come jogging with me before breakfast?

a) *Matthew:* ....

....

Douglas: I don't know why you think it isn't good for you. And as for it being bad for the heart, that's nonsense – it hasn't done mine any harm.

b) *Matthew:* ....

....

Douglas: Keep-fit classes? They may not cost much but jogging doesn't cost anything. Anyway, I don't feel like doing exercises after a day's work.

c) *Matthew:* ....

....

Douglas: I don't care if they have special classes on Saturday afternoons, I always watch football on Saturdays.

d) *Matthew:* ....

....

Douglas: I don't care what they say about dieting being the best thing. I don't want to give up all those things. I love starchy foods.

e) *Matthew:* ....

....

Douglas: Well, you do both those things and let's see who's lost the most weight in a month's time.

SECTION B

6   *Read the information given below about cars, and about Ted Wright, Camilla Bannister and Geoff Taylor. Decide which car would be most suitable for each of these people and give your answers, with reasons, in the space provided. Each answer should be in about 60 words.*

Ford were always pioneers.
We haven't changed much have we?

Today you're asking for cars that are better made, more efficient and kinder for the environment.

That's a challenge that Ford of Britain is eager to meet.

Because we're still an innovative company and we still care passionately about the quality of our products and the contribution they can make to the quality of life. Whilst never forgetting that driving should be enjoyable.

We hope you'll agree that we're on the right road.

This is only part of the Ford story. If you want to read more about it, pick up the latest issue of the Ford Cars catalogue at your nearest Ford dealer.

The Ford Sierra, 1984. An efficient aerodynamic beauty that's a pleasure to drive, it soon became one of Britain's best selling cars. Over half a million have already been sold. Man and machine in perfect harmony.

Ford is still in aviation, or should we say aerospace. Did you know Ford designed and manned the Computer Systems in NASA's famous Mission Control. With technology like that to call on, no wonder our cars are efficient.

Production line 1984. Robots help us achieve a consistently high quality of manufacture, by coping with the more dirty and difficult jobs with super-human precision.

Wind-tunnel testing 1984. Aerodynamic design is no longer a passing fashion. It's here to stay. Ford's own full size tunnel has taken it into the computer age.

The Escort Cabriolet 1.6i 1984. 0-60 in 9 seconds. Maximum speed 116 mph. The draughts have gone, but the driving is more fun than ever.

Popular in 1984. Today's Fiesta Popular is a comfortable, quick and safe little hatchback. Value for money is still a Ford forte.

A classic of the future? Probe IV may look like a dream car. But one day it might come true.

Ford cares about quality. *Ford*

TED WRIGHT:
– aged 46
– factory worker
– married, with two children
– needs a car for holidays and going to work

CAMILLA BANNISTER:
– aged 32
– executive
– single
– drives to the country frequently and likes a fast car

GEOFF TAYLOR:
– aged 57
– Head of an engineering company
– married, children grown up
– does a lot of business driving and entertaining clients

I think that Ted Wright ....

....

....

....

In my opinion, Camilla Bannister ....

....

....

....

It seems to me that Geoff Taylor ....

....

....

....

PAPER 4   LISTENING COMPREHENSION (20 to 30 minutes)

FIRST PART

Fill in the information you hear on the application form below. Some of it has been filled in for you.

Department of Extra-Mural Studies   Central Course

Application Form

Course number ①.................................... Fee enclosed ②......................

Course title .... *Drama & Theatre Studies* ....

If there is an examination involved, do you intend sitting it?   Yes/~~No~~

Surname ~~Dr/Mr/Mrs/Miss~~/Ms ③.......................................

First names ④...

Address ⑤...

....

Tel. no. daytime .... evening ⑥.......................

Occupation ⑦........................... Age ⑧...........................

Educational qualifications (if any)...... *B.A. English Literature* ......

⑨...

Previous extra-mural courses attended ⑩.......................

....

SECOND PART

For questions 11–15 tick (√) which you think is the correct answer in each case – A, B, C or D.

11 According to the interviewer, the high sales of computers indicate that

    A   the computer has now become the 'slave' of the household. | A |

    B   people are beginning to appreciate that modern inventions are useful. | B |

    C   machines are becoming the masters of households. | C |

    D   personal relationships will inevitably suffer. | D |

12 According to Susan, her brother and father are becoming 'computer junkies' because they

    A   think computers are going to take over the world. | A |

    B   always use the computer together. | B |

    C   like sorting out problems on the computer. | C |

    D   don't seem to care about anything but computers. | D |

13 Christine, the mother, can't understand why

    A   her husband prefers the computer to her. | A |

    B   it's not possible to joke with computers. | B |

    C   the computer doesn't respond like a real person. | C |

    D   the computer has got a lot of buttons to press. | D |

14 Susan began to dislike the computer intensely because

    A   computers are beginning to dominate the world. | A |

    B   her father wanted to work out programs on it. | B |

    C   it was taking her father away from her. | C |

    D   you can't talk to a computer about what's worrying you. | D |

15 We know Alec is fascinated by his computer because he

    A   won't allow the family to use it. | A |

    B   spends all his money on it. | B |

    C   spends all his time with it. | C |

    D   can't imagine life without it. | D |

THIRD PART

16 *Put a tick, as shown in number 10, against each picture which correctly shows that stage in the instructions for making an origami (paper) house.*

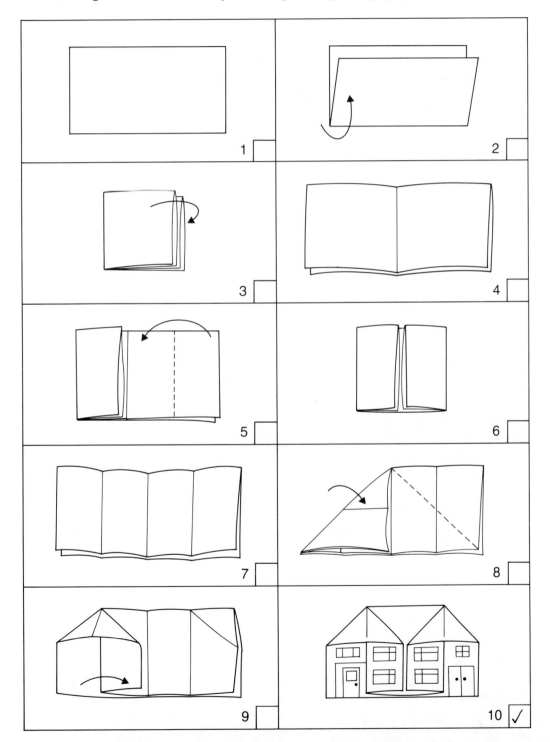

Test Five

PAPER 5   INTERVIEW (12 to 15 minutes)

SECTION A: PICTURE CONVERSATION

Look at this picture carefully and be prepared to answer some questions about it.

(See Teacher's Edition for suggested questions and topics.)

SECTION B: READING PASSAGE

Look at this passage and be prepared to answer some questions about it and then to read it aloud.

Now, if an article breaks soon after you have bought it, don't start to repair it. Take it back to the shop you bought it from and complain and ask them to put the fault right. Remember, anyone who pays for goods or services has certain rights and protection under the law. If the goods you returned are found to be faulty then you can demand your money back.

(See Teacher's Edition for suggested questions.)

SECTION C: STRUCTURED COMMUNICATION ACTIVITY

There may be a variety of options offered in this section. Choose one of the following:

a)   Prepare to give a short talk, to be followed by questions and discussion, on ways to learn a foreign language. You may write down some headings to remind you of the different ideas and options you wish to cover.

b)   Group or pair work.

Imagine that you and your friends are going to have a holiday in the mountains, you will be staying in remote mountain huts, miles from the nearest villages. Consider what equipment and food and clothes you will need to take with you. Remember you will have to carry everything with you as you climb the mountains.

c)   (See Appendix : Prescribed texts)

Appendix: Prescribed Texts

Candidates may choose one of the questions on prescribed books as a basis for one topic in Paper 2 (Composition) and one for Paper 5 (Interview). Prescribed books will vary from year to year.

Candidates should be reminded that only **one** of these topics can be chosen for Paper 2 (Composition). The other must be selected from topics 1–4.

The following are examples of the kind of topic the candidate may be asked to deal with on prescribed books:

ZERO HOUR

COMPOSITION (Paper 2)

Basing your answer on your reading of the book, answer **one** *of the following (between 120 and 180 words).*

a) Tell the story of Ha'penny as though you were Mrs Betty Maarman *or* Ha'penny himself.
b) Contrast any two of Thurber's fables and explain their morals.
c) Explain why Eric reacted so violently to the Pig-man and the possible cause.
d) Say which of the stories about a good little girl you preferred and why.
e) Explain the father's attitude towards the Maoris and say what effect their return had on him.

INTERVIEW (Paper 5)

a) *Consider the photograph opposite in connection with* Zero Hour *and show the relationship with the title story.*

b) *Study the following passages and be prepared to comment on one or more of them with reference to the characters, scenes or plots of the stories.*

   i) I am seventeen years of age, and left school two years ago last month. I had my A certificate for typing, so got my first job, as a junior, in a solicitor's office. Mum was pleased at this, and Dad said it was a first-class start, as it was an old-established firm. I must say that when I went for the interview, I was surprised at the windows, and the stairs up to the offices were also far from clean.

ii)   'Did you tell your wife you saw a unicorn?' asked the police. 'Of course not,' said the husband. 'The unicorn is a mythical beast.' 'That's all I wanted to know,' said the psychiatrist. 'Take her away. I'm sorry, sir, but your wife is as crazy as a jay bird.' So they took her away, cursing and screaming, and shut her up in an institution. The husband lived happily ever after.

iii)   Why, why had he gone on telling himself these lies, living a life of hypocrisy? It was as if he had been drugged – or was it simply that the air was so thick with nonsense, with cant, that it was almost impossible for any man to see the truth, even the biggest, the most obvious truth? Wasn't it simply by a stroke of luck that he had broken out into clear air?

c) **General discussion**

Choose one or more of the following questions about the book for discussion.

i)   In what way was the Pig-man important to Eric?

ii)   Why do you think the children preferred the bachelor's story to the aunt's in 'The Story-Teller'?

iii)   Why did the boy's father in 'The People Before' finally lose interest in his land?

UNIVERSITY OF CAMBRIDGE
LOCAL EXAMINATIONS SYNDICATE

Answer Sheet

PAPER 1   READING COMPREHENSION

NAME ....

PLEASE READ THESE NOTES CAREFULLY

1.   Check that this answer sheet has your correct name and index number printed on it.

2.   For each question, suggested answers are given on your question paper. CHOOSE ONE LETTER ONLY for each question, and show your choice clearly ON THIS SHEET.

MARK HEAVILY

EXAMPLE: If you think B is the right letter for Question 1, fill in the answer sheet like this

A ⌷   B ⬤   C ⌷   D ⌷

FILL IN THE LOZENGES

3.   **USE ORDINARY PENCIL ONLY** (SOFT - 2B or GRADE 1 PREFERRED)
     Any errors must be thoroughly rubbed out using a clean eraser.

	A	B	C	D			A	B	C	D			A	B	C	D
1	⌷	⌷	⌷	⌷		16	⌷	⌷	⌷	⌷		31	⌷	⌷	⌷	⌷
2	⌷	⌷	⌷	⌷		17	⌷	⌷	⌷	⌷		32	⌷	⌷	⌷	⌷
3	⌷	⌷	⌷	⌷		18	⌷	⌷	⌷	⌷		33	⌷	⌷	⌷	⌷
4	⌷	⌷	⌷	⌷		19	⌷	⌷	⌷	⌷		34	⌷	⌷	⌷	⌷
5	⌷	⌷	⌷	⌷		20	⌷	⌷	⌷	⌷		35	⌷	⌷	⌷	⌷
6	⌷	⌷	⌷	⌷		21	⌷	⌷	⌷	⌷		36	⌷	⌷	⌷	⌷
7	⌷	⌷	⌷	⌷		22	⌷	⌷	⌷	⌷		37	⌷	⌷	⌷	⌷
8	⌷	⌷	⌷	⌷		23	⌷	⌷	⌷	⌷		38	⌷	⌷	⌷	⌷
9	⌷	⌷	⌷	⌷		24	⌷	⌷	⌷	⌷		39	⌷	⌷	⌷	⌷
10	⌷	⌷	⌷	⌷		25	⌷	⌷	⌷	⌷		40	⌷	⌷	⌷	⌷
11	⌷	⌷	⌷	⌷		26	⌷	⌷	⌷	⌷						
12	⌷	⌷	⌷	⌷		27	⌷	⌷	⌷	⌷						
13	⌷	⌷	⌷	⌷		28	⌷	⌷	⌷	⌷						
14	⌷	⌷	⌷	⌷		29	⌷	⌷	⌷	⌷						
15	⌷	⌷	⌷	⌷		30	⌷	⌷	⌷	⌷						

SHOW YOUR ANSWERS ON THIS SHEET   **USE PENCIL ONLY**